APPLIED NLP WORKBOOK

A NEUROLINGUISTIC PROGRAMMING TRAINING & PRACTICE MANUAL

ANA MARCELA DUARTE

BALBOA.
PRESS
A DIVISION OF HAY HOUSE

Balboa Press books may be ordered through booksellers or by contacting:

Balboa Press
A Division of Hay House
1663 Liberty Drive
Bloomington, IN 47403
www.balboapress.com.au
1 (877) 407-4847

ISBN: 978-1-5043-0385-9 (sc)
ISBN: 978-1-5043-0386-6 (e)

Print information available on the last page.

Balboa Press rev. date: 08/17/2016

"NLP is the epistemology of returning to what we have lost – a state of grace."
John Grinder

Contents

BASIC - PRACTITIONER LEVEL NLP

CHAPTER 2 – MODELLING 167

Preface

I wrote this book as my way to contribute to Making the World a Better Place.

"Anything that engages people is worth doing"

Acknowledgements

My three trainers: George Faddoul, Tim Hallbom and Nick LeForce. I acknowledge them and thank them for providing me with World Re-known Leading Edge NLP Training and Coaching, for sharing their knowledge and their experiences without hesitation and for providing materials in the form of Training Videos and Seminar Notes which I have consulted many times throughout the years. I have used and adapted many techniques for the reader from their materials.
I thank them for their uninterrupted assistance, tenacity and belief in me.

I am grateful for all the supervised coaching experience I have had whilst coaching at seminars for the past 9 years which has lead to my sound knowledge in NLP and NLP Coaching.

I would also like to extend my gratitude to my family and to all my good friends including my many social media friends and followers for their witty advice and constant and unselfish reminders to stay fit and keep working on my NLP book for publication, for their moral support and help making my dream come true – to share this much needed knowledge and experience with the World in the most user-friendly form.

A BIG THANK YOU also to all those brilliant souls that came before us, paving the way and leaving behind their trail of study that we make use of today, a big thank you for their hindsight and foundational grounding/groundbreaking knowledge which makes precedence and sets the foundations for what we learn today.

Mission & Vision

This Manual is intended to be an easy to read – Applied NLP Workbook that will assist and guide the reader through Practitioner and Master Practitioner practice and TOWARDS Mindfulness and Proactivity, and going beyond coping in the world of today. This Manual can be used for self study but can also be used to train students in NLP and the many techniques and practices of NLP.

Perfecting ourselves by identifying and addressing our own incongruencies and working on ourselves and assisting others to communicate effectively, expressing ourselves and collaborating, whilst evolving spiritually, artistically and intellectually and exploring new ways to address the world's incongruencies is the aim of this book.

Many have said you cannot change the world but you can change yourself, if we all did this we would be changing the world, so maybe this is the way to change the world.

All techniques can be applied both on self and others.

(Incongruence: is when you don't walk your talk, when you are out of rapport with yourself and your unconscious mind, when you have reservations, doubts, inner conflicts and disharmony regarding an outcome, when you have internal conflict and cannot be totally committed to an outcome, and this will show up in your external behaviour. It may come up sequentially, as in saying something and doing something else, or simultaneously as in agreeing verbally but disagreeing physiologically with your head movements or doubtful tone of voice. Incongruence occurs when two or more of your programs are not in alignment, as opposed to being congruent when goals, thoughts, and behaviours are all in alignment...)

Understanding that 'The Map is not the Territory' is also important, I remind you that every person has their very own Map of the World, their own Map of Reality. Each person has a unique model of the world or their representation of the world we live in built from their own individual perceptions and experiences that lead to their internal representations. What each person holds to be true to them is their very own perception of reality....

NLP's 'Law of Requisite Variety' says: A person or a system with the most flexibility of behaviour will ultimately be the controlling element in the system....

In NLP when we talk about 'Leading' we mean changing/altering our behaviour or changing our physiology with enough rapport so that others follow.

There is so much you will love about this book and I hope you find it helpful in turning yourself into a TURNKEY SOLUTION in the unleashing of your true potential because if you are not a part of the solution, you are a part of the problem :P

Mission: The Mission or Goal is Evolutionary Mindsetting

Vision: The Vision or Outcome is that of a Better World,
one that improves and evolves without hostility.

I invite you to join me in this Journey of preparedness

so that we can ready ourselves and others to achieve our

Vision - a Better World, one that improves and evolves without hostility

This is

Our Greatest Legacy

How this Book Should Be Read

This book should be read in the order it has been written from beginning to end since even though you can decide to learn choosing a topic that interests you, many exercises will include the practice of prior knowledge and so you will need to have learnt certain skills to fully understand them. Many exercises are adaptations from my three trainers: George Faddoul, Tim Hallbom, Nick LeForce.

Understanding

To consider yourself proficient to some degree, I recommend you practice demonstrating / describing NLP concepts, methods and understandings analytically, conceptually, procedurally, interactively, judgmentally and relationally.

Feedback

There will be many instances for you to put on your self-discovery hats and experience things for yourself. This book will provide many opportunities for self-exploration.
Once you have read this book thoroughly and practiced the exercises you are welcome to ask me any questions via email and I would be more than happy to answer them

My Email Address is: AppliedNLPWorkbook@gmail.com

Disclaimer

Whilst this Manual may provide many valuable practical approaches to illness and disease, it in no way advises anyone to discontinue their therapy with psychologists or psychiatrists, and it in no way replaces a visit to your medical doctor. It in no way replaces treatment of any kind.

"A Culture of Excellence Awaits You"

Ana Marcela Duarte

BASIC - PRACTITIONER LEVEL NLP

CHAPTER 1

INTRODUCTION

QUOTES TO LIVE BY

"Awareness in and of itself is curative"
Fritz Pearls

"We are Co-Creators"
Esther and Jerry Hicks

"Awareness in and of itself is evolutionary"
George Faddoul

"The path to SUCCESS is to take massive, determined ACTION"
Anthony Robbins

"We can only exceed someone's expectations when we have managed to exceed our own"
Ana Marcela Duarte

"THE MAP IS NOT THE TERRITORY"

"The concept that the map is not the territory is one of the ideas that laid the foundations of Neurolinguistic Programming. It means that your understanding of the world is based on how you represent it – your map – and not on the world itself."
Tony Robbins

Our Maps either empower us or limit us,
with NLP our goal is to increase the chances of our language empowering us.
George Faddoul

"It all depends on how we look at things, and not on how they are themselves."
Carl Jung

WHAT NLP STANDS FOR

N – Neurology	N is for the mind and how we think. The neurology of the mind through which our experience is processed via our five senses (VACOG).
L – Linguistics	L is for how we use language and how it affects us. Language serves to code and give meaning to our internal representations through our language and other non-verbal communication systems including Pictures, Sounds, Feelings, Tastes, Smells and Self Talk.
P – Programming	P is for the sequencing of our actions to achieve our goals. (Strategies) Our Patterns and repeated actions, the automatic systems we use, including our communication with others and with ourselves in our neurology to achieve our outcomes.

NLP'S MANY DEFINITIONS

I think the best way to define NLP is: "NLP is the epistemology of returning to what we have lost – a state of grace." John Grinder

However there are many definitions, all different all valid:

- "NLP is an attitude which is an insatiable curiosity about human beings with a methodology that leaves behind it a trail of techniques." Richard Bandler
- "NLP is an accelerated learning strategy for the detection and utilisation of patterns in the world. John Grinder
- "NLP is an attitude and a methodology which leave behind a trail of techniques." Richard Bandler & John Grinder
- "NLP is the study of Human Excellence." Anthony Robbins
- "NLP is whatever works" Robert Dilts
- "NLP is the systemic study of human communication." Alix Von Uhde

NLP is also said to be the study of the structure of subjective experience, the influence of language on our mind and subsequent behavior, the method for Modelling excellence so it can be duplicated, the study of subjective experience and how it affects our behavior, the art of using language with such specificity as to create any fabric of reality, the How to use the mind's own language to consistently achieve desired outcomes, the ability to discover and utilise programs necessary to achieve our specific outcomes, and so much more but I think we now have an idea of the importance of NLP and the effect it can have in our lives.

It is difficult to pin down NLP to a single definition. There are a great many explanations of NLP and each one is like a beam of light shining from a different angle. NLP studies outstanding individuals and organisations, where they get their outstanding results from and the methods that can be taught to others so that they too can benefit from the same results, this process is called Modelling.

THE NATURE OF NLP

"The strategies, tools and techniques of NLP represent an opportunity unlike any other for the exploration of human functioning or more precisely, that rare and valuable subset of human functioning known as genius." John Grinder

"The greatest personal limitation is to be found not in the things you want to do and can't but in the things you've never considered doing" Richard Bandler

"If you think you can do a thing or think you can't do a thing, you're right." Henry Ford

"A goal without a date is just a dream." Milton Erickson

"You have to set goals that are almost out of reach. If you set a goal that is attainable without much work or thought, you are stuck with something below your true talent and potential." Steve Garvey

"All our dreams can become true if we have the courage to pursue them." Walt Disney

"The future is a good place to get interested in because you're going to be spending the rest of your life there." Paul McKenna

"Imagination rules the world." Benjamin Disraeli

"Whenever you want to achieve something, keep your eyes open, concentrate and make sure you know exactly what it is you want. No one can hit their target with their eyes closed." Paulo Coelho

"Change is the only constant in life. Are you going to choose the direction life will take and the kind of person you will become or will you just sit back and wait for life to happen to you?" Richard Bandler

NLP can also be said to be the study of excellence that was created to answer one simple question: How can I do whatever I am doing even better?

Just like physics studies the structure of the atomic world, and chemistry studies the structure of the molecular world, NLP studies the structure of our mental and emotional world.

Just like the laws of physics apply to anything made of atoms and the laws of chemistry apply to anything made of molecules, the laws of NLP apply to anything made of thoughts and emotions; so, if you want to be and do anything more successfully, whether building a business, healing your body, or reaching enlightenment, NLP has concepts, models and techniques to help you.

The core principle of NLP is that success and failure are not random.

Our thoughts, our feelings, our behaviours, our beliefs, our environment and our values create success and failure, and, the reason we think, feel, behave, believe the way we do is because that's what we were taught directly or indirectly by our families, schools and cultures.

There is no fixed lot in life, everything is changeable and most of it is *easily* changeable - our environments, our behaviours, our capabilities, our beliefs, our values, even our identity and spiritual purpose are changeable.

DOESN'T GENETICS LIMIT WHAT WE CAN DO IN THIS LIFE?

Certainly genetics forms an important part of who we are. If our glands produce more adrenaline, then we will have more energy; if our brain forms synapses faster, we will learn faster…On this level, genetics certainly is important, but pick any skill or ability, and any handicap that you believe you have, and, If we can find among six billion people on our planet someone with that handicap who excels at that skill or ability, then we can excel at it too.

NLP studies brilliance and quality, it studies how outstanding individuals and organisations get their outstanding results and these methods can be taught to others so they too can get the same class of results.

CAUSE OR EFFECT?

Are you living your life at cause or at effect?

How in control are you?

I learnt about cause and effect a few years ago at an NLP Seminar and it absolutely changed my life.

Before discovering 'cause and effect' I used to be the kind of person that stuff just happened to, I was living my life in victim mode allowing others to be in complete control of my happiness (or lack of) and I blamed everyone around me when things went wrong.

Being at cause means that you accept complete responsibility for what happens in your life and you take responsibility for your current circumstances. Being at cause you create the life you want for yourself by seizing opportunity and if things aren't going your way, you take action and make changes. When you are at cause you call the shots, you make choices about how you react to people and situations.

I'm not always at cause but I am at cause most of the time. In those moments when I do find myself at effect, I simply remind myself that I am in control and that I have choices. I make a plan and move forward – After all, there's no failure, only feedback!!!

With NLP there is so much we can do, so much we can change. Let's have a look at the NLP Communication Model and discover how we function.

THE NLP COMMUNICATION MODEL

Following is how we represent the NLP Communication Model:

Information => Senses => Filters => IR <=> State <=> Physiology => Behaviour

NLP began as a model developed by John Grinder and Richard Bandler of how we communicate and interact. The NLP communication model explains how we process the information that comes in from outside us and what we do with it inside.

There are some steps involved in this processing of information:

- First we are bombarded by around 2 million pieces of information per second.
- Information comes into our system /neurology/mind via our 5 senses.
- Our minds have some safety features, one of which is filtering and it is the way of reducing the information we are bombarded with down to a level that we can process.
- Filtering happens through our Filters (Time/Space, Matter/Energy, Language, Memories, Decisions, Meta-Programs, Values and Beliefs, and, Attitudes).
- After going through our Filters information is turned into our Internal Representations.
- Internal Representations combine with our Physiology to create our states

Our minds take in and process information and in turn this drives our behaviour.

The mind can handle 7 bit's of information (plus or mins 2).

INTERNAL REPRESENTATIONS

Internal Representations include our internal pictures, sounds, dialogue, feelings, tastes and smells.

An event comes in through our sensory input channels and is filtered and managed by our neurology. As we manage the perception of the event, we delete, distort, and generalise the information according to processes (Deletion, Distortion and Generalisation) that filter our perception.

MAJOR PRESUPPOSITIONS OF NLP

"Science like art, religion, commerce, warfare, and even sleep, is based on presuppositions."
Gregory Bateson

Presuppositions allow us to put a framework around NLP putting us in the best frame of mind to achieve a desired outcome.

There will be exceptions to all Presuppositions, but they are a very useful starting point for communication and personal development and working with clients.

It is important to have all Major Presuppositions in mind before an Intervention, throughout it, before and during our attempt to establish Rapport, and in developing and maintaining good Client/Practitioner relationships as well as in any other relationship that we consider important enough to maintain.

Here are some of the main ones:

- Communication is redundant.
- The meaning of your communication is the response that you get.
- The Map is not the Territory.
- Requisite Variety. (Behavioural Flexibility)
- People work perfectly.
- People always make the best choice available to them at the time.
- Every behaviour is useful in some context.
- Choice is better than no choice. (Important in Requisite Variety)
- Just about anyone can learn to do anything.
- People already have all the resources that they need.
- There is no such thing as failure, only feedback.
- Chunking - Anything can be accomplished by anyone if you break the task down into small enough chunks.
- Behind every behaviour is a positive intention.
- Symptoms – pains, anxiety, depression, tumours, colds, etc, are communications about needed action.
- We are all responsible for creating our own experience.
- Energy flows where attention goes.
- Respect the fact that everyone lives in their own unique model of the world.
- Life, mind & body are one system. You are in charge of your mind, and therefore your results.
- Resistance indicates a lack of Rapport. There are no resistant Clients, only inflexible communicators.
- If what you're doing is not working, do something else, do anything else.

- Experience has structure.
- Intention & behaviour are different. Accept the person, change the behaviour.
- Perception is reality, perception is projection, perception is a construction.

NLP STANDS ON SEVERAL CORE BELIEFS

NLP stands on several core beliefs. These are highly useful in everyday life and are held by most successful people. They help in creating the kind of life that we all want to live.

Following are some core beliefs we should keep in mind.

- People respond to their map of reality, not to the reality itself.
- Energy flows where attention goes.
- Behind every behaviour is a positive intent.
- People always make the best choice they can at the time.
- Choice is better than no choice.
- Anyone can do anything given the right strategy.
- There is no such thing as failure, only feedback.
- The meaning of the communication is the response you get.

WHAT IS THE LAW OF REQUISITE VARIETY?

The Law of Requisite Variety reads:

> "A person or a system with the most flexibility of behaviour will ultimately be the controlling element in the system".

The Law of Requisite Variety refers to behavioural flexibility or the ability to vary one's approach in order to achieve a desired outcome rather than having only one, habitual, limiting response.

Choice is better than no choice and three or more choices give us flexibility.

THE SIX MODALITIES OF CALIBRATION

The six modalities of Calibration are: Visual, Auditory, Kinaesthetic, Olfatory, Gustatory, and Auditory Digital.

Calibration is the ability to notice and measure changes with respect to a standard usually involving the comparison between two different sets of external, non-verbal cues.

By comparing, we are able to notice the difference between person's, places, things, states and behaviours.

Calibrating depends on refined Sensory Acuity.

Calibration, is the skill of learning to read unconscious, non-verbal responses.

SENSORY ACUITY AND WHY IT IS IMPORTANT

Sensory Acuity is what we call the ability to make more and more refined sensory distinctions in order to identify slight differences in what is observed, heard and felt.

Sensory Acuity acts as a radar system that helps the observer/Practitioner Monitor Client Progress and provides the observer/Practitioner with a sense of direction regarding whether the Practitioner is on track with techniques and other resources in general being utilised and whether or not the desired outcome is being achieved.

Robert Dilts defined Calibration as: "The process of learning to read another person's unconscious, non-verbal responses in an ongoing interaction by pairing observable cues with specific internal response."

Sensory Acuity is important because it's use is essential in the process of Calibration, the process of using sensory acuity to compare two pictures noticing the differences by reading unconscious signals such as voice tone, skin colour, micro muscle movements, and gestures that would indicate an internal shift.

More importantly, Sensory Acuity is purely observational and it has nothing to do with Judgement and evaluation.

We are always communicating something even if we are not using words or doing anything.

Having a well-developed sensory acuity enables the observer/Practitioner to notice things that other people would not notice in a Client's external dispositions that represent internal shifts.

Some external symptoms are:

1. A colour shift, usually face or neck - The skin and will usually go from lighter to darker or appear flushed.
2. A change in skin tone - The skin tonus may go from tight to relaxed.

3. Whether or not their face is symmetrical or asymmetrical.
4. The breathing rate may alter going either from normal to fast, or from normal to slower.
5. The breathing location may move - Visual people generally breathe higher up in the chest, auditory people breath more towards the middle of the chest, and kinaesthetic people breath lower in the diaphragm. When there has been an internal physiological shift due to an emotional reaction of some kind, the position of the breathing of all three groups will change. Establishing whether the person is predominantly a visual, auditory or kinaesthetic person is therefore determined in this way, which is information that the person's eye pattern movements does not provide. A deviation from this will be an indication that there has been an internal shift.
6. Lower lip size change - An internal shift can manifest in the lower lip getting fuller.
7. Pupil dilation - A person's pupils may be smaller or larger as they dilate depending on the internal changes that have occurred.
8. Muscle movement - Minute muscle movements can provide the Practitioner with feedback on the effects of communication.

Sensory Acuity is a valuable tool which enables the Practitioner to stop mind reading and have more accuracy in calibrating by criteria rather than by guess work.

SENSORY BASED VS HALLUCINATION

Hallucination in NLP is a sensory experience of something that does not exist.

Exercise:

Decide which of the following are Sensory Based (S) and which are hallucinations (H)

Her lips puffed.

He looked cold.

She was relieved.

His pupils dilated.

He showed remorse.

The muscles on her face tightened.

The volume of his voice was lowered.

CHAPTER 2

DEVELOPING RAPPORT

WHAT IS RAPPORT?

Rapport as we know, is a process that helps build trust, cooperation, harmony and responsiveness in relationships. It is also an extremely important skill when working in a Client/Practitioner relationship and it aids in the Client feeling in sync, or on the same wavelength with the Practitioner.

Rapport is established by matching, mirroring and cross-over mirroring Physiology (Posture, Gesture, Facial expression and blinking and Breathing), Voice (Tone, Tempo, Timbre, Volume) and Words (Predicates, Key words, Common experiences and associations, and Content chunks).

MIRRORING TO DEVELOP RAPPORT

MIRRORING is a technique based on mirroring the gestures somebody does, and it happens automatically when we're around people we feel comfortable with. There are many things that can be mirrored: Body Posture, Hand Gestures, Facial Expressions, Weight Shifts, Breathing, Movement of Feet and Eye Movements.

Over the years, other less obvious techniques for establishing Rapport with others have been discovered, Matching being a more successful and less obvious technique in developing Rapport.

MATCHING TO DEVELOP RAPPORT

MATCHING is simply doing what the other does and is more subtle than mirroring; if a Client puts his right leg over his left, the Practitioner does the same. (When matching, it is recommended to first focus on body language, then voice and finally the person's words.) It is though still quite noticeable.

THE FIVE THINGS YOU CAN MATCH TO DEVELOP RAPPORT

PHYSIOLOGY (55%)

- Posture
- Gesture
- Facial expression
- Blinking
- Breathing

TONALITY (38%)

- Voice Tone (pitch)

  Intonation Patterns:

  - W=>W=>up W Question?
  - W=>W=>W Statement.
  - W=>W=>down W Command!
- Tempo (speed)
- Timbre (quality)
- Volume (loudness)

WORDS (7%)

- Key words
- Common experiences & associations
- Content chunks
- Related Terms
- Predicates (Predicates in NLP are words and phrases (primarily verbs, adverbs and adjectives) that often presuppose one of the Representational System.)

For words, match predicates. Also consider using the same words as the other Client.

USING MISMATCHING TO BREAK RAPPORT

It is very important to learn how to break Rapport to end communication.

Mismatching can be used to break Rapport and we achieve it by using different patterns or contradictory responses regarding behaviour or words to interrupt communication.

It is easy to break rapport by breaking eye contact, turning your body at an angle, breathing faster or slower in contrast to someone's breathing or just doing anything to break Rapport by mismatching and you will find that quickly and easily the conversation will draw to an end.

CROSS-OVER MIRRORING TO DEVELOP RAPPORT

CROSS-OVER MIRRORING is said to be the most effective method in developing rapport since it consists of taking one aspect and matching it with another of our own. Cross-over Mirroring is choosing to match one of your behaviours to a corresponding, but different movement of another.

Here are some examples on how to develop Rapport using Cross-Over Mirroring:

- Use your hand movement to pace another person's breathing.
- Move your foot to pace another person's head movements.
- Tilt your shoulders slightly as the other person tilts their head.
- Lift a finger as the other person lifts an eyebrow.

Exercise:

Create your own crossover mirroring techniques and practice them.

USING GENUINENESS TO DEVELOP RAPPORT

GENUINENESS involves having a genuine interest in the person you are communicating with.

Intuition will be enhanced as we become aware of behaviours and actions that we were previously unaware of.

If the process intrudes into the other person's conscious awareness they may not feel comfortable so we need to be genuine without intruding into the other person's conscious awareness.

USING THE BACKTRACK FRAME TO DEVELOP OR MAINTAIN RAPPORT

The Backtrack Frame can help in gaining Rapport through pacing the content and the predicates of the Client's statements while we ensure we understand the Client's statements.

USING THE AGREEMENT FRAME TO DEVELOP OR MAINTAIN RAPPORT

The Agreement Frame can also help in establishing Rapport since it aims at disagreeing with the Client without upsetting them. Following are three examples of the Agreement Frame in use:

A. I appreciate 'that you believe'................
B. I respect 'that you believe'..............
C. I agree 'that you believe'............

Flexibility is important for effective communication; avoiding resistance from Clients/others keeps them involved in what one has to say and leaves them open to new ideas.

Avoiding negations like "but" and "however" in communication eliminates resistance, the agreement frame allows one to talk of differing viewpoints without growing resistance or compromising one's own values and beliefs.

PACING AND LEADING

Being able to pace and lead is very important in the process of establishing Rapport. While pacing what we do is that we set up a response pattern of what's true in the other person's mind. Human beings are creatures of habit, we like what's familiar, the human brain seeks patterns, and, having established a pattern, wants it to continue so when the brain has said 'that's true' three times, it's likely to say it for a fourth time.

Pace => Pace => Pace => - Lead

CHAPTER 3

REPRESENTATIONAL SYSTEMS

EYE PATTERNS OF A NORMALLY ORGANISED RIGHT HANDED PERSON

Eye Accessing Cues in NLP can be detected in the movement of the eyes. The eyes will move in certain directions that indicate that they are processing/thinking visually, auditorily or kinaesthetically.

The six areas the eyes will go to in order to find information are: visual remembered (top right as you are looking at them); audio remembered (middle right as you look at them); self talk, or calculations (lower right as you look at them); visual constructed (top left as you look at them); audio remembered (middle left as you look at them); tactile (lower left as you look at them).

The following are questions that a Client can be asked to identify their Lead Representational System and how they store information.

Visual Remembered Images.

What is the colour of the shirt you wore yesterday?

Which of your friends has the shortest hair?

Visual Constructed Images

What would your room look like if it were painted yellow with big purple circles? Can you imagine the top half of a tiger on the bottom half of an elephant?

Auditory Remembered - sounds or words

What does your best friend's voice sound like?
Which is louder, your door bell or your telephone?

Auditory Constructed sounds or words

What will your voice sound like in 10 years?
What would it sound like if you played your two favourite pieces of music at the same time?

Auditory Digital (Referred to as Internal Dialogue)

What is something you continually tell yourself?
What are your thoughts about this article?

In NLP we say Internal dialogue is the channel people use to 'beat themselves up', reinforce limiting beliefs and generally stop themselves having more fun in their lives, so it's nice to know that you can get more control over it & make it quiet.

Kinaesthetic - feelings (also smell and taste)

What does it feel like to walk barefoot on a cool sandy beach?
What does it feel like when you rub your fingers on sandpaper?

Exercise:

1. Find someone you don't know and begin asking questions
   (Questions are to be organised into sets to make the task simple.)

2. Start out by asking visual questions.
   (These are questions about things that the Client has seen before.)

   - What colour are the carpets in your car?
   - What colour are your mother's eyes?
   - What shape are the letters on the sign on the outside of this building?

3. Then ask questions about things that the Client has not seen and will have to construct.

   - How would you look from my point of view?
   - How would you look with purple hair?

4. Then ask auditory questions.

   - What's your favorite kind of music?
   - Which door in your house sounds the loudest when it's slammed?
   - Can you hear somebody very special that you are close to saying your name in a particularly delightful way?
   - Can you hear yourself sing "Mary Had a Little Lamb"?

5. Then ask a set of kinaesthetic questions.

   - How do you feel early in the morning?
   - What does cat fur feel like?

6. Once you have determined their eye accessing cues notice how they move their eyes while having a conversation.

LEAD AND PREFERRED REPRESENTATIONAL SYSTEMS

Our habitual eye movements are related to our lead and preferred representational systems.

A Client's preferred representational system is the sensory modality (visual, auditory, kinaesthetic, auditory digital) they use to organise and understand their experiences.

If we asked a right-handed Client with an auditory digital lead representational system 'What is the colour of your front door?', the Client's eyes would first go down to the left (auditory digital) before going up to the left (visual remembered), because the first thing they would do is repeat the question and make sense of it (auditory digital), and then get the answer (visual remembered).

If a Client's lead system is visual and we were to ask them "What does it feel like to be in a nice warm bath?", they would probably get a picture of being in the bath (visual remembered) before accessing the feeling.

The following quotes are passages taken from Richard Bandler and John Grinder's book Frogs to Princes.

"Your ability to perceive is something that is learned and you can learn to do it better." Richard Bandler and John Grinder

"Most people act as if their senses are simply passive receptacles into which the world dumps vast amounts of information. There is a vast amount of information, so vast that you can only represent a tiny fraction of it. You learn to actively select in useful ways." Richard Bandler and John Grinder

"We're making the claim right now that you've missed something that was totally obvious. We're claiming that you have been speaking to people your whole life and they've been going "Well, the way it looks to me..." (looks up and to his left), "I tell myself..." (looks down and to his left), "I just feel..." (looks down and to his right)—and you haven't consciously noticed that. People have been doing this systematically through a hundred years of modern psychology and communication theory and you've all been the victims of a set of cultural patterns which didn't allow you to notice and respond directly and effectively to those cues." Richard Bandler and John Grinder

USING EYE PATTERNS TO ASSESS TRUTHFULNESS OR CONGRUENCE

If a person is describing something that they have seen or heard, their eyes will move to visual or auditory remembered, however, while if a person is making something up, their eyes should move to visual or auditory constructed, indicating that they are constructing some part of the situation they are describing and it might indicate that the person is uncertain or untruthful about what they are saying.

THE LEAD REPRESENTATIONAL SYSTEM AND HOW WE DETECT IT

The Lead Representational System is the system used by a Client to access stored information. Watching their Eye Assessing Cues discovers the Lead Representational System.

THE PRIMARY REPRESENTATIONAL SYSTEM AND HOW WE DETECT IT

The Primary Representational System, often called the Preferred Representational System is the representational system that someone most often uses to calculate experiences and show them to the world, and is the representational system that we commonly and most easily employ. It is detected by predicates and body language, predicates being the words and phrases, primarily verbs, adverbs and adjectives that often presuppose one of the Representational Systems and body language being an important part of communication which can constitute 50% or more of what we are communicating.

Exercise:

Identify whether the following Predicates are Visual (V), Auditory (A), Kinaesthetic (K), Olfactory (O), Gustatory (G), or Auditory Digital (Ad).

Predicates	
Stink	(O)
Tension	(K)
Push	(K)
Watch	(V)

Music	
Throw	
Bitter	
Tough	
See	
Yummy	
Look	
Sense	
Thoughtful	
Tell	
Warm	
Putrid	
Shocking	
Silent	
Hard	
Motivate	
Brilliant	
Look	
Hear	
Remember	
Feel	
Taste	
Viewpoint	
Survey	

ESTABLISHING RAPPORT BY MATCHING PREDICATES

In NLP, Predicates are words and phrases (primarily verbs, adverbs and adjectives) that often presuppose one of the Representational Systems.

In order to establish Rapport by matching predicates we must first identify the predicate types that the Client uses and if they are using mainly visual words in order to establish Rapport we must use mainly visual words, and similarly for auditory, kinaesthetic and auditory digital words.

We should always try to use the same words as the Client.

Exercise:

Determine the Representational System of the following sentences:

Sentence	Representational System
Things look good.	(V)
Things sound good.	(A)
Things feel good.	(K)
Things have a good feel to them.	(K)
I think things make sense now.	(Ad) Internal Dialogue
Things sound good. Things have a good feel to them. Things are on track. Things are looking good. Things are starting to seem good.	
Everyday feels great! Everyday looks great!	

You are really fired up! You really sound enthusiastic. You look stunning!	
That sounds like a great idea. That looks like a great idea. That idea makes good sense.	
That appears to be a great idea. That sounds like a great idea. I have a good feeling about that idea.	
You really resonate well with me! You and I are starting to see the light! You and I have hit it off right! You and I get along great!	
People don't see me as I see myself. People don't get me. People don't grasp what I am trying to say. People don't seem to understand me. I think people don't think of me as I think of myself.	

Your words leave me without feeling. Your words leave me speechless. Your words make no sense. Your words draw no picture. Your words don't help me see the truth. Your words are of no help to make sense of it all.	
Everyday above ground is a great day! Position yourself smartly/wisely and you will see the light. Everyday above ground sounds like a great day!	
It is so quiet that you can hear a pin drop. It is so quiet that you can't see a soul.	
Your words leave a sour taste in my mouth. Your words strike me as very unpleasant. I think your words are very unpleasant.	
Others view me differently than I view myself. Others don't understand me. Others don't think of me as I do.	

OVERLAPPING REPRESENTATIONAL SYSTEMS AND WHEN TO USE THE TECHNIQUE

In NLP, Overlapping Representational Systems is moving from the Preferred Representational System or the one which is most predominant to another Representational System.

The process of Overlapping commences with pacing in the Client's preferred representational system and then leading them in another representational system.

If someone is predominantly visual you would start by talking in their language, in their predominant representational system and then move across to other representational systems as necessary, to provide them with more flexibility and then show them something they are missing.

CHAPTER 4

OUTCOMES

THE SEVEN KEYS TO ACHIEVABLE OUTCOMES OR WELL-FORMED CONDITIONS

In NLP, the ability to create and maintain an outcome that meets certain Well-Formedness Conditions is an essential application. Well-Formedness Conditions are the set of conditions required to produce an achievable, compelling and verifiable outcome.

In NLP, a Well-Formed Outcome is stated in the positive, self initiated and maintained, sensory-based, well contextualised as to whom, where & when, has a clear evidence procedure, has access to resources and is ecologically sound and it sets the scene for the rest of the game, and the level of attention given to plotting the outcome has a direct bearing on the ease with which desired results are achieved.

A Well Formed Outcome makes the difference between wanting something in theory, and becoming able to achieve it.

A Well Formed Outcome describes something that it's user wants in sensory based, positive terms including a description of what the user wants it for as well as the terms, conditions and environmental contexts in which they want to have it and includes consideration of different approaches to the outcome, time frames, costs and consequences to interested parties, and whether it is within the user's control.

In NLP, Ecology is important, it is the word used to describe whether an outcome has acceptable costs, time frame, and consequences including benefits.

We should always ask ourselves if the outcome is worth the effort, time and other costs involved in getting there, including strain and inconvenience on valued third parties, and if the end result is worth having and keeping; if it supports or detracts from the owner's chosen life style, relationships, and other factors that matter to them? If the time frame fits? If all the necessary resources are available to bring the project in to the chosen time and cost scale?

Most Clients have a less than sensory based idea of what they want the Practitioner to do for them, and if this process is used at the briefing stage, we can save them, and ourselves a great deal of time.

When we accept instructions from someone else, our outcome is to provide them with their outcome.

By answering the following questions we arrive at a Well Formed Outcome.

We can use the following questions to arrive at our own Well Formed Outcome and our Client's well formed outcome. Lets just work on our outcome and what the questions for achieving a Well Formed Outcome for ourselves would be (we can ask the Client the same questions formulated for them such as 'What do you want?' instead of 'What do I want?' and so forth):

1. What do I want?
   We must ask ourselves this question about the context we are considering and state what we want in positive terms, What do I want?, What do I want it to do? Where do I want it? When do I want it?

   (If the answer forms as 'I do not want...' then ask, 'What do I want instead of... ?')

2. Is it achievable?
   Is it possible for someone to achieve the outcome? Has it been done by someone before?, if so then it can be done by you, too.

3. What will I accept as evidence that I have achieved my outcome?
   What evidence will you accept that will let you know when you have the outcome?

   It is important to ensure that your evidence criteria are described in sensory based terms (what you can see, hear and/or touch that proves to you and/or third parties that you have done what you set out to do.).

4. Is achieving this outcome within my control?
   Is it under your control, can you, personally do, authorise or arrange it?

   If it is outside your control it is not 'well formed'.

5. Are the costs and consequences of obtaining this outcome acceptable?
   We must ensure that the outcome is worth the time, outlay and effort involved in achieving it, and that the impact on third parties or the environment is accounted for.

6. Do I have all the resources I need to achieve my outcome?
   It is important to consider if you have or can obtain all the resources, both tangible and intangible that you need to achieve your outcome, including knowledge, beliefs, objects, premises, people, money, time.

7. If I could have it now, would I take it?
   This is known as the Ecology Step. Consider the costs, consequences, environmental and third party impact of having the outcome.

The ability to create and maintain an outcome that meets certain Well-Formedness Conditions is an essential application of NLP and is easier seen like this in order to be able to describe what one wants in sufficient detail to be able to recognise it when it happens.

KEYS TO ACHIEVABLE OUTCOMES

In NLP we say "Our Outcomes should be BIGGER than our DAILY CONCERNS".

Following is a set of questions that the Practitioner can ask the Client to guide them through picturing their outcome clearly and getting them focussed and working on their outcomes.

- What is the outcome you desire?
- How is it possible that you don't have it already?
- When you think of your outcome do you have a picture?
- Stated in the positive, what specifically do you want?
- How has the picture changed?
- Specify your present situation. Where are you now in relation to your outcome?
- How has the picture changed?
- Specify your outcome. What will you see, hear, feel, etc, when you have it?
- How has the picture changed?
- How will you know when you have it?
- How has the picture changed?
- What will this outcome get for you or allow you to do?
- How has the picture changed?
- Is your outcome self initiated and self maintained? Is the outcome for you, first?
- How has the picture changed?
- Is your outcome appropriately contextualised? Where, when, how and with who do you want it?
- How has the picture changed?
- What resources are needed? What do you have now and what else do you need to get your outcome?
- Have you ever had or done this before?
- Do you know anyone who has?
- Can you act as if you have it?
- How has the picture changed?
- Is your outcome ecological? For what purpose do you want this?
- Has the picture changed?

IDENTIFYING CONGRUENCE AND INCONGRUENCE

- If you are serious about achieving your goals make sure you are congruent in all areas of life.
- Outcome review and readjustment/change it
- It is not my way or the highway but "A HIGHER WAY"
- Only grade yourself against your potential, this is where meaningful competition comes from.

THE PHYSIOLOGY OF EXCELLENCE AND WHY IT IS IMPORTANT

The Physiology of Excellence is the physiology we model from others who are excellent in their field.

NLP was created as a result of Modelling.

Bandler and Grinder's system for Modelling essentially discovers somebody's belief systems, physiology, and mental strategies by eliciting a successful person's internal program, which they called "mental syntax", or "strategy" and copying it to develop excellence in self.

PERCEPTUAL POSITIONS

In NLP, the application of Perceptual Positions is known to enhance understanding and aid in communication and is a technique used in problem solving, mediation and negotiations in general.

- How do I feel about a situation…..
- Then step into "other" – What can you learn from this position.
- What about "observer" – What else are you picking up now, which might make all the difference.

Modelling successful people is truly important if our aim is to become successful and there is no need to "Reinvent the wheel".

SUCCESSFUL PEOPLE DO THINGS THAT FAILURES DON'T DO.

Successful people are outcome oriented and have goals, they focus on what they want, they ask questions, they are good listeners, they learn (knowledge is power), they think for themselves, Identifying the possibilities and taking the responsibility of making the decisions to create life their way for their own reasons instead of making up excuses for why their life is not the way they want it. They are sensible risk takers and they stretch their comfort zones.

SEVEN EASY STEPS FOR EMPOWERING ONESELF

1. Ask Yourself: What Do I Want?
2. Ask Yourself: What is Stopping Me From Getting What I want?
3. Deal With Your Doubts.
4. Deal With Your Limiting Beliefs.
5. Find Out What Your Current Situation Does For You.
6. One Step At A Time
7. Play A Bigger Game

NLP FIVE PRINCIPLES FOR SUCCESS

The FIVE PRINCIPLES FOR SUCCESS are also known as THE FIVE PILLARS OF NLP and they are:

- Know your Outcome
- Take Action
- Have Sensory Acuity
- Have Behavioural Flexibility
- Time and Rapport

SMART FORMULA

Our outcomes should be:

- Specific
- Measurable
- All encompassing, All areas, As if now - How is one area of life impacting the others.
- Reasons, your reasons (Reasons not Excuses – C/E)
- Timed

CIRCLE OF CRYSTALS TECHNIQUE

Imagine laying out a circle of crystals on the floor right in front of you (It needs to be big enough to step into, about 2 feet in diameter)

Take a moment to relax, clear your mind and breathe deeply.

Then take in the power of the crystals:

The power of Jade to experience unconditional love with everyone you come into contact with.

The power of Aventurine to release fear and anxiety and create a positive attitude towards your life.

The power of Ctrine to feel and experience abundance in all aspects of your life.

The power of Amethyst to allow divine love to flow through you bringing its calming healing touch.

The power of Carnelian to become one with your inner self and experience the joy in opening your heart.

The power of Sunstone to feel free from the stress of everyday life and have the vitality of the sun.

The power of Howlite to communicate well with all and make your time of rest peaceful and deep.

The power of Rose Quartz to let go of all your past anger and resentments and forgive others with love and compassion.

The power of Pyrite to find working with others a simple matter and turn all negative vibrations into positives.

The power of Agate to find levels of strength and courage that you had hidden from yourself.

The power of Rhodonite to feel confident in everything you put your hand to.

The power of Tiger Eye to have excellent insight in all your dealings, personal or business.

The power of Clear Quartz to allow yourself the joy of total energy, rejecting all negative thoughts and patterns from your life.

The power of turquoise to strengthen your friendships with communication and loyalty.

The power of Flourite to find concepts easily grasped and your concentration being at a maximum.

The power of Jasper to feel the benefits of total grounding, becoming one with your surroundings.

And the power of Obsidian to feel you are alive with energy and change negative energy into positive in a stress free way.

Absorb all the energy that the crystals have to offer and intensify it.

Stand, breathe and feel the sensations.

Step out of the circle energised and ready for the day.

Everyone should have a Circle of Crystals, remember to step into your Circle of Crystals whenever you need to. Having this resource will affect all aspects of your life in a positive way.

CHAPTER 5
STATES

WHAT IS 'STATE' AND WHY IT IS IMPORTANT

In NLP we say a State is how a person feels internally and it relates to our internal emotional condition.

In NLP we believe that the state determines our results, and so we aim at being in states of excellence.

In NLP, our Internal Representations, plus our State, and our physiology results in our Behaviour.

A State is different to an Outcome – if a person tells us that they want to be happy – happiness is a state not an outcome and they can become happy straight away (use of resource/happiness anchor).

In NLP, Resources are the means to create change within oneself or to accomplish an outcome. Resources may include certain states, adopting specific physiology, new strategies, beliefs, values or attitudes, even specific behaviour.

A State is also important because we are constantly anchoring states even when we don't know it.

The anchoring of states is used as part of many techniques in NLP. Following we will see a State Elicitation Script.

STATE ELICITATION SCRIPT

- *Can you remember a time when you were totally **happy and excited?***
- *A time when you felt totally powerful?*
- *A time when you felt totally loved?*
- *A time when you really felt you could have whatever you wanted?*
- *A time when you felt you couldn't fail?*
- *A time when you felt you could have it all?*
- *A time when you felt really energetic, when you had a ton of energy?*
- *A time when you fell down laughing?*
- *A time when you felt totally confident?*
- Can you remember a specific time?
- As you go back to that time now... go right back to that time, float down into your body and see what you saw, hear what you heard, and really feel the feelings of being totally **happy and excited.**

This is the script used when anchoring a state. Also, if we want to extend this exercise and find resources in the past we use an anchor to take us back to other similar states and we stack anchors, but we will see this further on.

WHAT IS A 'BREAK STATE' AND WHEN WOULD WE USE IT

In NLP, a break state is a sudden change in the context of speaking or movement that changes a person's state quickly and we use a break state to change a person's state.

An example could be to make up a picture in your mind, once you have done this, open your eyes and clear your mind by stretching and looking around the room. In NLP, this is called a break state.

Another example is, doing some exercises on the floor and breaking state by standing up and stretching and looking around the room.

Breaking the state is very important in NLP as it serves to leave one state behind and enter into a 'neutral state' or another state. This helps to reduce or even stop the residue or contamination from one state to another.

People sometimes find it difficult going from one state to another, especially if they are both powerful <u>states</u>. The break state acts as a stepping stone, a bridge that is neutral to both states.

Any question implies a Break State

- "Do you play golf?"
- "Can you smell popcorn?"
- "Do you like meatballs?"

WHAT IS A 'PATTERN INTERRUPT' AND WHEN WOULD WE USE IT

In NLP, a Pattern Interrupt is the method of breaking into a pattern, breaking into the behaviour to change the behaviour at the end.

We use a pattern interrupt to change a person's behaviour.

Pattern Interrupts are useful because they allow for the restructuring of a different behavior; the interrupt becomes part of the new behaviour.

A Pattern Interrupt interrupts a behaviour; it is anything you do in the middle of a behaviour before it goes funny. Every time a behaviour starts that you know will end up in unresourceful behaviour and you know where it is going to go and that it's not going to take you to where you want to go use a pattern interrupt. For example a pattern interrupt can be used in a conversation before it turns into an argument. Anything that will change the direction of the conversation can be used as a pattern interrupt.

CHAPTER 6
FRAMES

FRAMES AND WHEN TO USE THEM

"There is nothing either good or bad but thinking makes it so."
William Shakespeare

In NLP, Framing is important because nothing has meaning in itself. We will find that Information does not exist on it's own but rather has to be understood in context since the meaning we derive from any experience depends on the frame we apply to it.

In NLP we say that because we are always framing, it is an essential step towards understanding and meaning. The frames we have govern the questions we ask about what happens, how we feel, how we react, and what we do. Questions are a powerful way of setting frames, because they include assumptions about an event.

Frames can even be made up of a single word…*Obviously*………, or, *Unfortunately*…….., or, *You*…………., or, *We*………………………………………

Framing, is a term used commonly in media studies, in sociology and psychology and it refers to the social construction of a social phenomenon by mass media sources or specific political or social movements or organisations. Framing is an inevitable process of selective influence over the perception of the meanings attributed to words or phrases.

A frame can define the packaging of an element of rhetoric in such a way as to encourage certain interpretations and to discourage others.

In NLP, a Frame is the particular point of view or the context around a specific experience and it provides a context or focus for our thoughts and actions in the same way that a picture frame puts borders or boundaries on what you can see in a picture, the frames of reference that we choose as a result of our beliefs about ourselves and others, our perceived role in life and our perceived limitations in skills and abilities can limit what we see as possible or can open up all sorts of possibilities.

We are continuously setting timeframes, boundaries, and limit's on what we can and can't do and many times we do this without any real thought about the consequences.

The way we look at a problem depends on the Frame we give it which can make it easier or harder to solve.

In NLP there are several well known Frames and we will see eight of them here now:

The Outcome Frame

In NLP, the outcome frame allows us to focus on the 'outcome' of a situation, driving the brain to find options for achieving that outcome. If we are problem solving, or negotiating, using the outcome frame sets the goal that we aim at achieving. It might help us by focusing on the purpose of a request. The question to ask here is 'For what purpose' making us focus on the existence of a purpose which will provide us with the information that we need.

The Outcome Frame evaluates events by whether they bring us closer or not to our outcomes. In order to apply the Outcome Frame we should judge every action in terms of whether it gets us closer to what we want or not. The Outcome Frame should not be used without reference to the Ecology Frame.

In NLP we say that the Outcome Frame can be used for day to day behaviours, and also as a way of planning what to do because It is not just a frame but a purposeful way of living.

The Outcome Frame can be applied by asking the following questions:

- "For what purpose?"
- "What are you trying to achieve now?"
- "What do you want?"
- "What does this get for you that is of value?"

The opposite of the Outcome Frame is the "Blame Frame"; using the "Blame Frame" puts us on the Effect side of the C/E equation rather than on the Cause side. We need to be on the Cause side which would indicate we are being resourceful/applying resourceful techniques.

The Agreement Frame

The Agreement Frame can help in establishing Rapport since it aims at disagreeing with the Client without upsetting them, three examples of the Agreement Frame in use are:

A. I appreciate that you believe.................
B. I respect that you believe..............
C. I agree that you believe............

Also known as the Agreement Frame or Mediation Frame is the useful skill of moving a person beyond a limiting, non-productive outcome and it is especially used where there is a conflict and where there are people unable to view each other's point of view.

It is known that when two parties rise above the level of a problem, they can reach quality agreements.

The Agreement Frame in this sense and for this purpose is more of a process with a number of steps:

First each person specifies their current frame, by listing the values, criteria and beliefs behind each goal. Gathering of important information from each individual occurs, making them both feel valued and heard.

Then all the common elements at the higher level that both parties agree on are identified.

In moving to a higher common level, both parties rise above their current personal levels.

The next step is to base the negotiation on the higher-level agreements where it is necessary to move back down to the specifics, and reach a compromise that is acceptable to both parties. The final step is to conclude and confirm the agreement, by identifying and solidifying every level of agreement and it's importance to each party.

The Evidence Frame

The Evidence Frame is a subset of the Outcome Frame and it asks the following questions:

- How will you know when you have achieved your outcome?
- What will you see, hear, feel or experience?

In NLP, the evidence frame is used to assess progression towards an outcome and to identify when the outcome has been achieved.

The Backtrack Frame

In NLP, Backtracking is the skill of restating key points using another person's own words, often their matching voice tone and language as well. It is a skill for pacing another person.

Backtracking questions are simple:

- "Can I check that I understand….?
- "Can I summarise so far?"
- "So you are saying that……?"

In NLP, the Backtrack Frame is useful for:

- Gaining Rapport through pacing the content and the predicates of a Client's statements.
- Making sure to understand a Client's statements.
- Giving the Practitioner time to think about what he/she is going to say next.

- Giving the Practitioner an opportunity to rephrase what another says and thereby change his/her experience.

The Relevancy Frame

In NLP, the Relevancy Frame is a statement of relevance used when a Client is on another train of thought that has nothing to do with the desired outcome. Then the statement of relevance returns them to what is being talked about.

The Contrast Frame

In NLP, the Contrast Frame evaluates by the difference that makes the difference.

There are many NLP patterns that use a Contrast Frame for contrastive analysis and they take one unresourceful situation and contrast it with a similar situation that was resourceful with the significant differences being used as resources and brought into the unresourceful situation.

The Contrast Frame is very easy to use because we naturally notice difference.

Questions for the Contrast Frame are:

- "How is this different?"
- "What is it that makes this stand out?"
- "What are the important variations between these things?"

The Ecology Frame

As we know, Ecology is the study of consequences towards system/environment and the focus is on how one thing affects everything (self, family, community and planet, career, business, industry, the world) so when a change passes the ecology test everyone benefit's – the person, the family, the organisation, the environment or system, everyone.

Ecology in NLP is the study of the consequences or results, the impact of any change that occurs on everyone and everything as a result of the change.

In NLP, a fundamental precept is to always leave someone in a better 'place' than before you started. It goes beyond the medical precept of 'First do no harm'.

In NLP, the ecology frame gives us the perspective of looking at the wider implications of any change that NLP generates. It makes us answer the questions of:

- Is this change going to improve this person's life?
- What is the impact on this person's family and business life?

- What will this new behaviour replace?
- What was being satisfied by the old behaviour and is it still being satisfied?
- Is the new state a Well Formed Outcome for this person?

In NLP, the Ecology Frame aims at long term, evaluating events in terms of wider meanings and looking beyond boundaries we would normally set in time, space and people.

Ecology frame questions are:

- "How will this be over the long term?"
- "Who else is affected?"
- "What would they think?"

The opposite of the Ecology Frame is the "Me Frame"

The 'As if' Frame

The 'As if' Frame allows a person to see the world 'As If' they had a skill, behaviour or resource.

In NLP, the intent of this frame is to make it easier for a person to explore possibilities and ideas internally, which would normally be unavailable to them due to their limiting beliefs about themselves or others and it allows a person's limiting beliefs to be temporarily set aside for the purpose of exploring alternate possibilities, without having to threaten or challenge their existing conceptual world-view in the process.

Questions to apply the 'As If' Frame are:

- "What would it be like if ….?"
- "Can you guess what would happen…..?"
- "Can we suppose that…..?
- "Let's imagine that ………………?"
- "Let's think of it as being ……………………?"

The opposite of the 'As If' Frame would be the "Helpless Frame". – "If I don't know, then there's nothing I can do about it."

FIVE MAIN NLP PROBLEM-SOLVING FRAMES:

"Outcome" rather than "Blame"

We've seen the outcome frame previously. To make any change we need to know:

- *Where we are now – present state.*
- *Where we want to be – desired state.*
- *The resources we need to move from one to the other.*
- *Our plan of action to narrow the gap between the present state and the desired state.*

Outcome Frame Questions are:

- *"Where are you now?"*
- *"What do you want?"*
- *"How can you get from where you are to where you want to be?"*

The opposite of the Outcome Frame is the Blame Frame. Outcomes look to the future, blame to the past.

"How?" rather than "Why?"

In NLP we say that to fully understand a problem it is necessary to see how it is being maintained in the present and why it hasn't dissolved.

'How' questions are generally more useful than 'why' questions in problem solving because they uncover the structure of the problem.

Questions to get the structure of the problem are:

- *"How has this problem been maintained?"*
- *"How has the way the situation has been set up contributed to this problem?"*
- *"How can I solve this problem?"*

"Possibilities" rather than "Necessities"

The outcome should be set by what we can do in a situation rather than what we cannot do or have to do.

Questions to uncover possibilities are"

- *"What is possible?"*
- *"What would have to happen for this to be possible?"*
- *"How could I make this possible?"*

"Feedback" rather than "Failure"

In NLP we say that our actions narrow the difference between our present state and our outcome.

We need to continuously monitor where we are to make sure we are on track for our outcome. This monitoring gives us the feedback we need and it's quality depends on what we measure, how we measure and how accurately and precisely we measure.

Feedback that let's us know we are off track is as useful as feedback that let's us know we are on the right track.

In NLP, when we are focussed on what we want we find that all results are helpful to direct our effort and that "failures" are simply short term results we did not want. Remember the NLP Presupposition "There are no failures only Feedback".)

Questions about feedback are:

- *"What are my results so far?"*
- *"What have I learned from them?"*
- *"What am I going to do differently as a result of that feedback?"*
- *"What feedback will let me know that I have succeeded?"*

"Curiosity" rather than "Assumptions"

In NLP, curiosity is important because it allows us to stay open to choice and possibility.

Assuming about a problem limits the range of solutions.

In NLP, there is a saying about assumptions that goes "If you always do what you have always done, you will always get what you have always got", and it is important to notice that when we assume, we do not ask questions, because we think we know the answers already.

Questions to uncover assumptions are:

- *"What are you assuming about the problem?*
- *"What are you assuming about the people involved?"*
- *"What has to be true for this to be a problem?"*

OTHER USEFUL FRAMES

The Cause and Effect Frame

In NLP we know that this frame allows a person to understand the relationship between what they are doing and the result they are getting, by adapting the mental filter of looking at how something we do causes an effect, we are getting near real time feedback about how we are influencing the world.

The cause and effect frame is used for instance during public speaking to see if the pitch, tempo and material is having the wanted effect. If not then it's time to change the approach until one gets the results wanted.

The Systemic Frame

In NLP, the Systemic Frame evaluations by relationship focussing not on single events but rather on their relationship to other events. We know that a system is a group of elements that are connected and that influence each other for purpose, so, when we apply this frame we are looking for connections and relationships.

We know that 'Systems Thinking' looks at how the factors combine and affect each other to explain what is happening, they are stable and they resist change, so when we apply the systemic frame we ask what stops the change and we concentrate on removing obstacles rather than acting directly to achieve the change we want. Whether you understand this or not, just try asking the following questions:

Systemic Frame questions are:

- "How does this fit with what I know?"
- "How does this connect to the wider system?"
- "What is the relationship between these events?"
- "What stops the change?"
- "How does what I am doing keep things as they are?"

The Negotiation Frame

In NLP, this frame is also known as the win-win frame and it evaluates by agreement assuming we are engaged in a negotiation and that everyone would prefer to come to an accord.

The Negotiation Frame assumes that coming to an accord is possible and that the resources are available.

The key question is:

- "What can we both agree on?"

It is important to notice here that the opposite of the Negotiation Frame is the "War" Frame – "I want something and I'm going to get it if it kills us.", this is what we don't want happening, we therefore need more win-win situations/experiences.

The Purpose Frame

In NLP, with the Purpose Frame we are meant to 'chunk up' or elevating a conversation to a higher level. When asking "for what purpose?", the neurology looks for a higher meaning automatically.

The key question here therefore is obviously "for what purpose" and looking for purpose and meaning in what we and others do is essential in living a more peaceful and agreeable life.

THE POSITIVE FRAME AND THE NEGATIVE FRAME

The Positive Frame

Positive Frames redirect a person's attention towards a positive aspect or implication of some situation.

The well known proverb "Every cloud has a silver lining" is a positive reframe because it redirects a person's attention towards a positive aspect or implication of some situation.

In NLP, a positive reframe implies a thought transition whereby a situation is evaluated in an improved/higher way.

The Negative Frame

"All that glitters is not gold" is another well known proverb and it is considered also a negative reframe as it redirects a person's attention towards a negative aspect or implication of some situation.

In NLP, a negative reframe also known as a loss frame can also be considered and used as a helpful warning about a situation that could get worse.

As we have seen, the distinction between negative and positive reframing applies to proverbs.

Positive frames have been found to be superior to negative frames in terms of pleasantness and they also might be more effective than negative frames in some cases. Positive reframes involve a thought transition to a positive and improved way of thinking whilst Negative reframes can be useful warnings.

CHAPTER 7

ANCHORS AND ANCHORING

ANCHORS AND ANCHORING

In NLP we know that an Anchor is an internal state that is triggered by an external stimulus.

Any time someone is in an associated, intense state, if they are at the peak of that experience a specific stimulus is applied linking the two neurologically forming what in NLP we call an anchor.

Anchors can be formed and reinforced by repeated stimuli, and thus are similar to classical conditioning.

There are different definitions of anchoring; here are a few versions from different well known people in the field of NLP.

Anchoring—"The process by which any representation (internal or external) gets connected to and triggers a subsequent string of representations and responses. Anchors can be naturally occurring or set up deliberately. An example of an anchor for a particular set of responses is what happens when you think of the way a special, much-loved person says your name." Tony Robbins

Anchor: "Stimuli that will consistently produce the same internal data in an individual. Anchors occur naturally. Bandler and Grinder discovered old Modelling that you can deliberately set-up a stimulus with a gesture or a touch or a sound to hold a state stable. Where an external stimulus is paired with an internal state." Robert Dilts

"An anchor is a representation--either internal as with a picture or feeling, or external as with a touch or sound--that triggers (elicit's) another such representation. It's a sensory stimulus paired with either a response or a specific set of responses or states." Michael Brooks

"In the same way that certain external stimuli become associated with past experiences (thus recalling the past experience) you can deliberately associate a stimulus to a specific experience. Once this association has taken place, you can then trigger the experience at will. It works in the same way that language does." Leslie Cameron-Bandler

"Anchoring refers to the tendency for any one element of an experience to bring back the entire experience." Bandler & Grinder

"….it is an NLP way of talking about classical (Pavlov's) conditioning." Sid Jacobson

"The way we naturally link things that happen at the same time. This knowledge gives us a way to take resources from one area of our lives and apply them in broader ways for our well-being." Steve Andreas

"People represent their inner worlds to the outside via a series of built in anchors; Andrew Salter remarked that we just jump from one reaction to another. What that means is we code our meaning via the associations we have made with them. If a certain look someone gives you is the look your father used to give you when you did something wrong, unless you have cleaned that up, you are likely to respond in the same way as you did with dad!" Terry Elston

Anchoring was first mentioned by William Twitmire from his work on the knee jerk response. Ivan Pavlov is the one most people remember because of the dogs and bells.

In NLP we say "Basic anchoring in essence involves the elicitation of a strong congruent experience of a desired state whilst using some notable stimulus such as touch, word or sight at the time this is most fully realised."

HOW AN ANCHOR DEVELOPS

We know that Anchors develop when two events happen together on a regular basis for a certain number of times and that an overly sensitive person is more likely to develop an anchor faster than anyone else. We know that anchoring is a process that goes on around and within us all the time, whether we are aware of it or not and more often than not, we are unaware of it so it happens out of our conscious awareness.

WHY USE ANCHORING IN NLP?

In NLP, anchoring is used to facilitate state management. An anchor is set up to be triggered by a consciously chosen stimulus, deliberately linked by practice to a known useful state, to provide reflexive access to that state at will and we now know it may be used for exam nerves, overcoming fear, feelings such as happiness or determination, or to recollect how one will feel if a good resolution is kept.

THE FOUR STEPS TO ANCHORING

1. Have the person recall a past vivid experience.
2. Provide a specific stimulus at the peak (can be a slight touch of the arm when the vivid experience is at it's peak)
3. Change the person's state. (Break State)
4. Set off the anchor to test.

Exercise:

Try to discover some of your own anchors, you may be surprised. Decide on whether they are positive or negative anchors.

THE FIVE KEYS TO ANCHORING

Following are the five keys to anchoring which we need to keep in mind when creating an anchor.

1. Intensity of the Experience
2. Timing of the Anchor
3. Uniqueness of the Anchor
4. Replication of the Stimulus
5. Number of times

In NLP, the best states to anchor are naturally occurring states; the next best are past, vivid, highly-associated states and the least preferable are constructed states but they can also be useful in many exercises so we must also consider them.

Exercise:

Try anchoring yourself to some positive states that you can use later. Once you have created the anchors test them.

STATE ELICITATION SCRIPT FOR STACKING POSITIVE ANCHORS

Anchors can be stacked; they are usually stacked in the same spot.

Following you will learn how the Practitioner elicits states and anchors them by slightly touching the Client's arm when the states are peaking. This is what the Practitioner will say:

- *Can you remember a time when you were totally_____?*
- *A time when you felt totally powerful?*
- *A time when you felt totally loved?*
- *A time when you really felt you could have whatever you wanted?*
- *A time when you felt you couldn't fail, when you could have it all?*
- *A time when you felt really energetic, when you had a ton of energy?*
- *A time when you fell down laughing?*
- *A time when you felt totally confident?*

- Can you remember a specific time?
- As you go back to that time now... go right back to that time, float down into your body and see what you saw, hear what you heard, and really feel the feelings of being totally _____.

THE PROCESS OF COLLAPSING ANCHORS EXPLAINED

The NLP technique of Collapsing anchors creates an anchor for the problem state that we want to change, and a second anchor for the positive state that we would rather have instead. (The positive anchor should be created first, it will replace the negative anchor once they are triggered together.)

By firing off both the anchors at the same time, particularly if the positive anchor and state is stronger than the negative we come to a new resourceful state exactly at the moment that we need it.

THE PROCESS OF CHAINING ANCHORS EXPLAINED

In NLP, Chaining Anchors is a sequencing of a series of states. If you have set up a few anchors, you can fire them off one after the other, changing the state as each emotion is peaking which will make you move through a sequence of states.

A useful anchor chaining process will make you go through the different states automatically, and so we can say that the first state will induce a process that automatically leads to the last state.

Chaining is a technique that is used when the desired state is different from the present state and the present state is a stuck state.

CHAPTER 8

TIME AND THE TIMELINE

HOW IS TIME STORED?

In NLP, a Timeline is the unconscious arrangement of our past, present and future memories, experiences, and outcomes and it is normally experienced as a line that stores our internal representations.

Our mind knows if a memory is from the recent or the distant past.

Our mind codifies memories so that it can differentiate between different dates and times.

It was recently discovered that we actually map out time in our 'minds eye', carrying with us a timeline from which we access memories and resources.

SCRIPT FOR ELICITING THE TIMELINE

Following is what the Practitioner would say to a Client:

1. Remember a time when you …………………………..about 5 years ago and notice where that image is located in space and point to it.
2. Imagine (doing something)…………………………………………. in the present and notice where you would place the image in space and point to it.
3. Finally imagine doing something 5 years from now and allow yourself to become aware of where that image would be located in space and point to it.
4. When you look at all three images at once you can imagine a connecting line between them. This is your timeline.
5. Looking at your timeline now where is your birth located and where is 25 years from now?.

USING THE 'AS IF' FRAME TO ELICIT THE TIMELINE

The 'As if" frame is sometimes also referred to as the 'Pretend' frame.

The 'As if' or Pretend Frame is used in saying things like:

"'pretend' to be one year in the future and having achieved certain goals" or

"Take a look back from the future and identify what steps you took to achieve that result"

We can see how from a new perspective we might identify some insightful points that were not available to us in the present.

The intent of this frame is to make it easier for a Client to explore possibilities and ideas internally, which may not be available to them due to their limiting beliefs about themselves or others.

The specific effect sought is to allow a Client's limiting beliefs to be temporarily set aside for the purpose of exploring alternate possibilities without needing to threaten or challenge their existing conceptual world-view in the process.

MODIFICATION OF A CLIENT'S TIMELINE

There are many techniques that have the focus on the modification of the Client's Time Line itself.

There are two types of timeline work based on whether we utilise the existing timeline or we change it.

We can change a traumatic memory on the timeline by reorienting in time, or by adding in resources; the structure of the Timeline itself can also be changed and in doing this kind of work, we find out in detail how a Client's Timeline is structured and what they want to have different in their life, and then we reorient the Timeline so as to support the kind of person they want to be.

Once the structure itself is changed, the Client will live in a new relationship to all their experiences in time - not just the traumatic ones, or the resourceful ones, but all of them.

Changing a Timeline is literally the process of reorganising all of a person's life experiences, so it must be done with extreme care and sensitivity. For instructions and examples on how to elicit and change Timelines the following books are recommended "Heart of the Mind', 'Change Your Mind and Keep the Change', and Connirae Andrea's videotape 'Changing Timelines' (1992).

CHAPTER 9

GETTING SOME BASICS RIGHT

BASIC OUTCOME SPECIFICATION

The Basic Outcome Specification criteria is basically just a way to take notes of a client's progress. It is used to keep track of or monitor progress and it is documented.

It might look something like this:

Present State Information

What is the unwanted Behaviour or State?

What are the contexts in which it occurs?

What cues trigger it?

What positive function might this behaviour serve?

What will need to be preserved?

Desired State Information

Outcome

- "What new Behaviour/State do you want?
- "Is it worth having? (ecology testing the wanted outcome)
- "What would that Outcome do for you?" (ecology testing the wanted outcome)

Evidence Procedure

- "How will you know you have it?" (What do you see and hear?)

Contextualisation

- "Where, when, with whom do you want it?"

There are also a wide range of techniques that we can use, BUT FIRST we need to do an ECOLOGY TEST, lets check Ecology.

CHECKING ECOLOGY

What we mean by Checking Ecology is evaluating the costs, consequences, environmental and third party impact of using one or more techniques to achieve a Client's Outcome.

The ecology frame gives us the perspective of looking at the wider implications of any change that NLP generates. It makes us answer the questions of:

Is this change going to improve this person's life?

What is the impact on this person's family and business life?

What will this new behaviour replace?

What was being satisfied by the old behaviour and is it still being satisfied?

Is the new state a Well Formed Outcome for this person?

"How will this be over the long term?"

"Who else is affected?"

CHAPTER 10

THE META MODEL AND THE MILTON MODEL

THE META-MODEL

The Meta Model is NLP's first formal model and was published in 1975 by Richard Bandler and John Grinder in a book called "The Structure Of Magic".

There are thirteen verbal patterns that constitute the Meta Model and they are a highly effective verbal model for use in the specific context of therapeutic change.

The Meta Model can be used to challenge the limitations in the mental maps (Deletions, Distortions and Generalisations) carried by Clients who seek professional assistance in changing themselves and is used to get Clients to expand and/or revise their mental maps that contain traps, flaws, and limitations that prevent them from communicating and behaving more effectively and congruently and this improves Clients' quality of life and the life of whom they communicate with/amongst.

IDENTIFYING META MODEL VIOLATIONS AND META MODEL CHALLENGES

The Meta Model Challenge is the so called Inquiry in search for missing information lost through Distortions, Generalisations and Deletions. Let's see some examples:

Sentence	Meta Model Violation	Meta Model Challenge/ Questions to ask	Predictions
I'm angry	Deletion/Simple Deletion: Simple Deletion	About what/whom? (What are you angry about? Who are you angry with? You are angry about........)	Recovers Deletion
Sue loves me	Distortion/Mind Reading	How do you know she loves you?	Recovers Source of the info
Susan hurt me	Distortion/Cause-Effect	How did what Susan did cause you to choose to feel hurt? How specifically?	Recovers the choice
It's wrong to cheat	Distortion/Lost Performative: Value Judgement where the person doing the judging is left out.	Who says it's wrong? According to whom? How do you know it's wrong? (It's wrong because.............)	Gathers evidence. Recovers Source of the Performative strategy for the belief.
I regret my decision	Deletion/Simple Deletion: Simple Deletion	About what? What decision do you regret? You regret your decision about......	Recovers Deletion

He makes me happy	Distortion/Cause-Effect	How does what he is doing cause you to choose to be happy? How specifically?	Recovers the choice
I should study harder	Generalisation/Model Operator: Model Operator Deletion/Simple Deletion: Comparative Deletion	What would happen if you did? didn't? Harder than whom? Harder at what? Compared to whom, what?	Recovers Effects, Outcome. Recovers Comparative Deletion.
Nobody ever pays any attention to me. I will never go near any fire ever again.	Generalisation/Universal Quantifier: Universal Generalisations	Nobody? Ever? Any? What would happen if they did? didn't? Never? Any? Every again? What would happen if you did? didn't?	Recovers Counter Examples, Effects, Outcomes

USING THE MILTON MODEL TOWARDS AGREEMENT

The Milton Model is an NLP model that can be used throughout an intervention towards agreement. It has many language patterns that can be used throughout an intervention and especially to end an intervention leading to agreement. We will see a few of them here:

Mind reading

"I know that you came here for a purpose."

"I know that you are determined to find a solution to your problem."

"I know how determined you are."

Conversational postulate

"Could you open your mind for a while?"

"Could you hold on to those thoughts?"

Cause and Effect

"You will become more relaxed as you feel the fresh air coming in."

"Because you are here you have taken the first step to feeling better."

"As you listen closely you will start to remember."

Exercise: Try coming up with some examples of your own.

Mind reading

....

....

....

Conversational postulate

....

....

....

Cause and Effect

....

....

....

CHAPTER 11
TECHNIQUES

TAPE EDITING TECHNIQUE

Tape Editing is a technique which is similar to how we do a video editing on a computer, there may be unclear shots or unwanted scenes which we don't want so we clip them leaving only what we want.

Those shots we want to clip in this case are all negative memories, feelings and behaviours so we stack negative anchors for each of them and then collapse them with a strong positive anchor which we prepare before doing the Tape Editing and can be considered the first step in Tape Editing.

THE SWISH TECHNIQUE

The Swish Technique is for dealing with negative or unpleasant thoughts and feelings about the Past (feelings from embarrassing or irritating memories), the Present (feelings provoked by self-undermining thoughts) or the Future (anxiety-provoking thoughts about forthcoming situations) and its all about replacing the image of the unwanted experience for an image of a more desirable experience. We call it the 'Swish' technique because the replacement is a quick one and we can imagine swishing from one image to the other with a Swish sound.

THE NEW BEHAVIOUR GENERATOR TECHNIQUE

The New Behaviour Generator Technique is an NLP technique that uses mental imagery and rehearsal, moving from vision to action, through which we can develop skills more easily. We learn through observation, practice and refinement. We've been doing this intuitively all of our life. One of the most essential processes of change is that of moving from a dream or vision to action. By choosing a Role Model and emulating them we can create a new behaviour. The very last step is the big test in a real life situation, where a Client needs to be convinced consciously that they have learned a new behaviour for this to be a success.

THE FAST PHOBIA TECHNIQUE

The Fast Phobia Technique is all about observing an experience as if it were a movie and watching it backwards and forewards in colour and then in black and white from different perceptual positions. The more detached we are from the unwanted experience the less emotions we will have attached to it turning it into a less meaningful experience. This is a process that must be done fast and the more we repeat the process the more likely to succeed at detaching ourselves or a Client from the unwanted experience.

THE BELIEF CHANGE TECHNIQUE

This technique is all about replacing the submodalities of a limiting belief with the submodalities of a belief that is no longer true and then to replace the submodalities of a belief they want to have to those of a belief that is true and always true like the sun comes out each day. Its all about submodality work and its quite easy to do.

METAPHORS AND STORYTELLING

A lot has been said about metaphors, many authors relate to metaphors as creative tools for communication. Judy Bartkowiak in her book 'Secrets of the NLP Masters' rightly says that in NLP we use the term 'metaphor' to describe analogies, jokes, parables and stories, similies and allegories and that it is an indirect way of communicating that bypasses the conscious mind and that used creatively and appropriately it can have more of an impact than speech because we conjure up images and mental pictures rather than being restricted simply by the meaning of the word.

"Metaphors can be enchanting, enticing and mesmerizing. There effects may be enlightening and empowering when they are developed and recounted constructively." Sue Knight

"Stories get to the parts that other words don't reach. They speak to you at an unconscious level. They enable you to convey information indirectly, to pace someone's current reality and then lead them on to a new one. To move away from problems to different outcomes. To open up new possibilities." Romilla Ready and Kate Burton

"Metaphors are not simply poetic or rhetorical embellishments, but powerful devices for shaping perception and experience." Nick Owen

"Metaphors illuminate some aspects of an experience while leaving other aspects in the shadows." James Lawley and Penny Tompkins

"All which is not concrete is metaphoric – clearly, this involves the vast majority of our everyday experiences. The structure of the unconscious – easily the most influential factor in our success in life – or more correctly said, the relationship which we have with our unconscious is easily the most important factor in our success in life – is that of metaphor." John Grinder

"The unconscious contains no nouns, only verbs – the part of language which carries the representation of the relationships and processes which determine the quality of our lives. This in part accounts for the fact that the typical production of the unconscious is metaphoric: dreams, poems, dances, songs and stories." John Grinder

TESTING & FUTURE PACING

Testing and Future Pacing occurs after the application of every technique:

TESTING – Practitioner asks: "Now how do you feel about that old state?"

FUTURE PACING – Practitioner asks:

"Can you imagine a time in the future when you might be in a similar situation, and what happens?"

Contextualise if necessary.

FIRST ASSOCIATED "See what you would see through your own eyes, feel what you would feel, hear what you would hear."

THEN DISSOCIATED "Now see yourself in the picture, what do you see, feel, hear."

CHAPTER 12

REFRAMING AND CLOSING

REFRAMING

When defining Framing we learnt that the meaning of an event depends on how we frame it. With Reframing what we learn is that when we change the frame, we change the meaning.

With Reframing we can change our representation or perception about something and in a moment change our states and behaviours. This is what reframing is all about.

Reframing enables us to put a new or different frame around an image or experience. What may seem like an extremely challenging situation in the present can be reframed to have less impact when considered as part of your whole life experience.

"We have the mental tools and skills to get rid of the crap we don't want and replace it with what we do want. You can be whoever you choose to be." Richard Bandler

"A signal has meaning only in the frame or context in which we perceive it." Tony Robbins

"Take that which you no longer need, bless it for what it has done for you, and then set it free." Virginia Satir

CONTEXT REFRAMING

In NLP, Context Reframing is giving another meaning to a statement by changing the context.

Context reframing takes an undesired attribute and finds a different situation where it could of value. Reframing in this way has the purpose of helping a Client experience their actions and the impact of their beliefs from a different perspective to become more resourceful and have more choice in how they react to situations.

A good question to ask when context reframing is: 'Where could this behaviour be useful?" or "In what other context would this behaviour be of value?"

VALUE REFRAMING

In brand management and marketing terms 'value reframing' means giving a new value to a product/service by finding a new market/context. This is done very often to find a new market for a product or service, targeting a completely new audience for the product or service being offered.

CONTENT OR MEANING REFRAMING

The content or meaning of a situation is determined by what we choose to focus on. To do a Content Reframe is to give another meaning to a statement by recovering more content, which changes the focus.

When to Content Reframe? When we find a C/E or Complex Equivalent.

In NLP we say "If you are experiencing a physical problem, phobias or allergies, try asking yourself if the problem is useful to you in some way or if there is some other way that you can get the same result without having to have the physical problem, phobia or allergy and as a result you might find that the physical problem, phobia or allergy disappears." Also, Content Reframing is about finding meaning in life and finding the lessons in experiences and a good question to ask ourself is 'What else could this mean?' or 'In what way, could this be positive or in what way could this actually be a resource?'

If we have a problem state for example we can ask ourselves "How is this a problem?" and then just ask ourselves:

A Context Reframing Question: 'Where could this behaviour be useful?" or "In what other context would this behaviour be of value?"

A Content Reframing Question: 'What else could this mean?' or 'In what way, could this be positive or in what way could this actually be a resource?'

THE SIX-STEP REFRAMING TECHNIQUE

In NLP, the Six-Step Reframe is a pattern for changing unwanted habit's and behaviours developed by John Grinder. It's purpose is to identify that every symptom or problem has a positive function behind it and change behaviours that a client wants to stop doing but can't. The Six-Step Reframing technique addresses behaviours that seem to be out of conscious control, it addresses that something we want to stop or change but seem unable to.

The Six-Step Reframing Technique can also be used when we are blocked from doing something that we want to do; not being able to change behaviour at a conscious level is an indication that there is secondary gain – the behaviour is getting us something that is important to us that we do not want to give up.

We use the Six-Step Reframe on unwanted habit's, sequential incongruence, physical symptoms, psychological blocks and secondary gain and we do this by finding the positive intention, a different way to satisfy the intention that we feel more congruent about and that is more ecological and in keeping with our sense of self.

If a client, when explaining his "problem" starts off with "I can't stop..........................." or "I want to ....but for some reason I can't seem to ...." you can use the Six Step Reframing Technique.

We identify a problem for example smoking, nail biting, anxiety, pain and discomfort when there is no overt physical cause. The Client will express it as: "I want to do this but something stops me..." or "I don't want to do this, but I seem to keep doing it just the same..."

Then we identify the positive intention and aim at finding new ways of fulfilling that positive intention, and using one or more choices rather than the original behaviour and we run an Ecology Check to make sure the new choice/es are ecological and then we Future Pace Imagining the new choices in the future.

The following are the basics of what the Client would be doing in the six step reframing.

- Thinking of something that they would like to stop doing.
- Thinking of what the positive intention of the behaviour could be?
- Thinking of what it is trying to achieve that is of value?
- Thinking of how else it could fulfill that positive intention?

THE AGREEMENT FRAME AND WHEN TO USE IT

As mentioned previously, flexibility is important for effective communication, if we can manage to avoid resistance from others we will find that it keeps them involved in what we are saying and leaves them open to new ideas.

We can go a long way toward eliminating resistance from others by avoiding negations like 'but' and 'however' in our communication.

We can disagree with a person or subject matter without upsetting them by using:

- I appreciate that......................and/but.................
- I respect that.......................and/but.......................
- I agree that............................and/but....................

The Agreement Frame can be used to pace and then lead into the Conditional Close Conditions.

THE CONDITIONAL CLOSE AND WHEN TO USE IT

In NLP, Conditional Close is a frame which helps determine from the outset what issues need to be satisfied before a solution can be finalised.

Exercise:

1. B (Practitioner) makes proposal to A (Client)
2. A raises an objection.
3. B backtracks A's objection.
4. **B makes the conditional close:**
   If I can satisfy your objection, then you would agree to 'X', is that correct?

5. If no, go back to step 2 and ask for all objections, then follow through the steps again.
6. If yes, you have an agreement!!!

The Conditional Close can be used on every occasion because the "The meaning of communication is the result we get."

CHAPTER 13

STRATEGY

STAGES OF COMPETENCE – THE LEARNING STEPS

1. Unconscious Incompetence => 2. Conscious Incompetence => 3. Conscious Competence =>

=> 4. Unconscious Competence

Whenever we learn a new task we first think about how we will start and the steps necessary to get to the desired result.

We start off at the unconscious incompetent stage unaware that we cannot do the skill until we attempt it for the first time and become conscious of our level of incompetence.

With practice and patience we become skilled but we still need to think about how we accomplish the task, and are consciously competent with the skill.

And finally we reach the stage where we don't have to think about doing the task or how we are doing the task. This is the final stage, the stage of unconscious competence.

WHAT IS A STRATEGY? - THE T.O.T.E. MODEL

The T.O.T.E. or TOTE Model stands for "Test => Operate => Test => Exit", and has been described frequently as an iterative problem solving strategy based on feedback loops.

It was described by George A Miller, Eugene Galanter, and Karl H. Pribram in their book *Plans and the Structure of Behaviour,* published in 1960, which outlined their conception of cognitive psychology.

Whenever we carry out a TOTE what we are really doing is:

T1 - Test – We ask ourselves if a strategy works and eliciting the steps involved.

O - Operate – We apply the strategy or sequence of IRs on self or other.

T2 - Test – We ask ourselves if we have reached our goal, if the results were as expected/positive. (and if positive we exit, if not we Exit and then find a new Strategy and ask ourselves again T1)

E - Exit – If the Strategy or sequence of IRs delivered a positive result then we Exit and this is the end of the TOTE otherwise as mentioned before we Exit and then go back to T1

Even though this suggests there is only a two-step loop I would like to explain that in order to be precise we need to see it as a sequence of T1=>O=>T2=>E and if T2 hasn't delivered positive results, only then we exit and reloop. Relooping is therefore then necessary if and only if T2 has not delivered the results expected proving the strategy did not work (on self or other).

As you may have noticed the first Test and the second Test, ie T1 and T2, are different. In T1 we are identifying a strategy that has already worked on someone else (it includes strategy elicitation) and in T2 we are getting the results of having run the strategy on self or other which will indicate whether we loop again or not after exiting).

This is my adaptation of the original T.O.T.E. Model and I believe it can be more easily understood explained in this way reflecting how it occurs more precisely.

WHY DO STRATEGIES MATTER?

In NLP, it is important to notice that we have programs for everything we do. These programs consist of sequences of thoughts and behaviours triggered by a stimulus.

In NLP those programs are called Strategies and they are therefore Internal Programs for Achieving Outcomes and if you know about the components of an internal processing strategy, you can change it, copy an effective strategy from somebody else, or create a new one from scratch.

In NLP we say "Strategies matter because they are the internal keys to success." If we're ineffective at something, chances are our internal strategy isn't working.

Ineffective strategies prevent people from achieving things like managing finances, giving presentations, communicating well with people at work, cooking, making decisions, maintaining positive and fruitful relationships, and more…

STEPS FOR ELICITING A STRATEGY

If we want to copy someone's strategy first we need to make sure we are copying from the best in the field so that we get a strategy that works.

In order to copy a strategy we first need to elicit the strategy from that person who is the best in the field.

When eliciting a strategy, we discover a sequence of thoughts and behaviour, as well as values, beliefs and meta-programs. The steps involved in eliciting a Strategy are as follows:

1. First choose a skill you would like to improve for example study skills (everyone has their own way of studying).
2. Find someone that is good at studying and elicit their strategy for studying.
3. Map out the strategy by finding the trigger or event that kicks off the process. Write down the strategy or steps that they go through. (Make sure you also write down the thoughts they think as well as how they feel.)

You might want to quickly run them through some of the following questions:

*   *How do you know when to do this?*
*   *What let's you know you are ready to do this?*
*   *What do you do as you are preparing to ….?*
*   *What steps do you go through?*
*   *What happens next?*
*   *Then what happens?*
*   *How do you know when you have succeeded?*
*   *How do you test whether you have succeeded?*
*   *What let's you know if you have not yet succeeded?*

4. Then check the Strategy, go through it to see if you've missed anything

THINGS TO REMEMBER WHEN WORKING WITH STRATEGIES

In NLP. Strategies can be improved, copied or created new; they are the recopies for success.

Strategy Elicitation can be used to figure out somebody else's strategy for success if we want to model them just as we have previously learnt.

When eliciting someone's Strategy for success at anything we need to identify the details of thoughts, feelings and actions; it's more than the mechanical act of performing a task.

Success depends on precision. Normally, we just notice behaviour. If we don't know the sequence of thoughts and the details such as the internal dialogue or visuals, we limit our success. This applies whether we're improving a strategy, copying a strategy or creating a new one.

Also, if we are seeking perfection and success in life, it is important to identify the strategies that work and don't for us. Our best habit's are our best recipes/our best strategies and we need to capture them for future use.

Our worst habit's are those we need to change and when we fully understand the pattern of our bad habit's we can use strategies to change them, we just need to change the recipe/strategy and make it more effective.

If we have a new skill that we want to learn or there is an area of your life where we might have potential but we need some strategies, we need to practice our strategy elicitation with someone who is successful at it and model them by doing what they do.

We need to only model the best in the field, so, we need to find mentors for something we want to be great at and practice eliciting the mentor's strategies and copy them ourself.

Equally important is to focus on the habit's that are holding us back as well as on the ones that will take our game to the next level. We need to think of what skills we might have that separate us from the pack and instead of trying to make all our good skills great try making a few of our great skills outstanding.

In NLP we say: "Always remember that if we're not succeeding, if we are not achieving the outcomes we want, then the solution can come in the form of a strategy change."

We can borrow strategies from the very best in the field who already have strategies that work.

Even though we might not realise it people have recipes or strategies for every type of behaviour including:

- Delight
- Depression
- Shyness
- Evaluation
- Motivation
- Procrastination
- Decision making
- Wealth

- Poverty
- Love

So, if we can find times when our clients are motivated, energised, excited, making good decisions and really firing, they can learn from these situations, copy the strategies and apply them to areas where they're less effective.

"By concentrating on precision, one arrives at technique, but by concentrating on technique one does not arrive at precision." Bruno Walter

Let's concentrate on precision!!!

PLANNING STRATEGY (STORYBOARDING)

This is an exercise that anyone can do even on their own. It will allow the Client to gain more insight into the three main positions of managing a project.

In every project you need a Dreamer, a Realist and a Critic. The Dreamer is who accesses, is inspired and sees the big picture; The Realist is who organises, is grounded and sets out the steps involved and the Critic is who evaluates, is wise and who critics the plan.

We need all three for any project but maybe we are on our own so we need to step into each of the three roles or positions. So basically this is all we need to do, step into each position or put on each of the three hats.

After we have repeated this cycle several times we need to continue to walk through the dreamer, realist and critic locations until our project or plan congruently fit's each position.

Exercise:

Use this planning strategy on a project of your own.

A STRATEGY FOR RESPONDING TO CRITICISM

In responding to criticism we need to first identify the type of criticism, it is not all negative and worthless, it is not all positive and resourceful either. There is good criticism from well meaning people, vague criticism, and criticism that has no information for future improvement and we need to identify what type of criticism we are receiving.

If we wish to approach criticism analytically we need to for example recall some recent criticism we received and analyse it. What type of criticism is it? We need to notice what the other person is saying and to compare what they are saying happened to what really happened. Then we need to agree with it or not and come up with an appropriate response to what the other person is saying and we can rehearse the response to the critic. Also it is important to acknowledge feedback and think through whether there is any behaviour you would like to change as a result of the criticism and if so rehearsing it and future pacing it.

Exercise:

Try evaluating criticism you have received. Do it as instructed to above.

CHAPTER 14

MEETINGS NEGOTIATION AND SALES

MEETINGS, NEGOTIATION AND SALES

There are so many of NLP's techniques that can be used for successful meetings, negotiations and sales.

NLP can be used for a wide range of situations to gather the right information, to develop rapport, to communicate with collegues and clients and to sell and especially to close sales.

Let's have a look at a few pointers...

FIVE NLP INSIGHTS INTO CONDUCTING A SUCCESSFUL MEETING

   a.   Determine the Outcome (Well Formedness Conditions)
   b.   Develop the Evidence Procedure (Evidence Frame)
   c.   Establish Membership and Agenda (Itinerary and listing of those invited –RSVPs)
   d.   Develop Options (Behavioural Flexibility)
   e.   Establish Rapport (If the meeting is a phone conference then matching of voice tone, speed of voice, predicates etc………..)

THE IMPORTANCE OF INTENT IN NEGOTIATION

In NLP, we know that Deep Structure is usually hidden and out of awareness. For the most part it is only the surface structure or thought that is freely shared with others and the underlying complete representation making up the deep structure is often unconscious, and people's behaviours are often guided by them.

In NLP we say: "Intention is the underlying deeper purpose or desired outcome behind a behaviour, assumed to be positive." Our intentions satisfy our outcomes in a way that is consistent with our beliefs about the actions that can cause outcomes to occur in the given context, and, where an outcome is a goal we wish to achieve, intentions refer to the behaviours which we intend to perform to achieve our outcomes.

We know that Intention is an invisible power or strength that is behind every action and that this intention has been produced from our "Map of The World".

In NLP, one of the Major Presuppositions reads "Behind every behaviour is a positive intention." This means that while a behaviour may be harmful or seem "bad" there is always a positive intention behind the behaviour.

The proper use of the Meta Model helps unravel the deep structure and brings it back into consciousness.

FIVE NLP TACTICS FOR NEGOTIATION

1. We need to determine our outcome with Well Formedness Conditions, SMARTS FORMULA, and having the Conditional Close determined.
2. We need to develop as many options as possible to achieve the outcome. (Flexibility)
3. We need to identify potential areas of Agreement, things we might have in common in order to share similarities and develop or enhance rapport with the other party.
4. We need to identify issues to be resolved and plan how to discuss them, thinking of alternatives or choices for flexibility.
5. We need to determine our best alternative to an agreement (Future Pacing and Testing it 'as if' then.)

Exercise:

Following Five NLP Tactics for Negotiation, write down the steps for negotiating something that is of interest to you.

NLP IS USEFUL IN SUCESSFUL SELLING

There are some key principles in sales and how to improve on them through the use of NLP.

Selling is simply the process used to:

- Take a person with a potential need to recognising their need
- Attaching value to the product or service offered to their needs
- Removing obstructions allowing them a clear thought process
- Encouraging them to make a decision and closing the sale

Behind this there need to be a few things that need to be in place for the process to work well:

- A respectable product or service
- The belief of the sales person in themselves
- A prospect with a need
- Knowing the product or service and confidence in the ability to deliver a product or service that fulfils the expectations of the buyer

For good clean and ethical selling all the above need to be in place.

Exercise:

Pretend you have a product or service to offer and follow the steps involved in the Selling Process mentioned previously. What would you write, how would you reach out to your audience?

THE IMPORTANCE OF VALUES

In NLP we say: "Values are the primary source of our motivation and they determine how we spend our time, and so they drive our actions."

Values in NLP are high-level generalisations that describe what is important to us.

In NLP, Values are sometimes called Criteria. Criteria or Values refers to the standards or values a person uses to make their decisions, evaluations and judgments about the world around them.

To elicit Criteria or Values the question to ask is "What's important to you about.....................?"

This can be useful when we are getting to know our Client. Knowing what they Value is very important.

Values are our "Evaluation Filter" through which we delete, distort and generalise information.

Our values constitute essentially an evaluation filter. They are how we decide whether our actions are good or bad, right or wrong and they determine how we feel about our actions.

Values are arranged in a hierarchy with the most important ones typically being at the top and lesser ones below that. We all have different internal models of the world, and our values are the result of our model of the world but they also define it.

Richard Bandler says, "Values are those things we don't live up to."

Values are what people typically move toward or away from. They are our attractions or repulsion's in life. Values are essentially a deep, unconscious belief system about what's important and what's good or bad to us.

Do you know your values?

Exercise:

Try listing 10 values you live by in point form and then try prioritising them from 1 to 10.

PUBLIC SPEAKING AND RELAXING

I have chosen to include the following two Scripts in this book because Public Speaking and Relaxing are two activities people need extra support on.

Public Speaking is something anyone with the skills and a bit of determination can do, the script is just here to help.

Relaxation is something we all need to learn to practice as it will improve our quality of life and the quality of our communication and relationships. I have included a relaxation script here to help you achieve full relaxation. There are also many tapes and books on the subject.

Always remember, where attention goes energy flows.

(If you wish to read them out to a Client all you need to do is change the verb tense.)

CHAPTER 15

SCRIPTS AND FUTURE GOAL SETTING

THE PUBLIC SPEAKING SCRIPT

"I enjoy public speaking because I love speaking to an audience and being heard, I love that the audience has something to learn from me and that what I am sharing is of interest to them. I love sharing and I love being heard. I speak clearly and am very confident.

I share my thoughts and what I have learnt and people listen to me, they listen to what I have to say, they listen to my opinions on various topics and they learn from what I am sharing. I find public speaking to be very exciting and rewarding.

I love people and I love sharing with them. I realise that my opinions matter to my audience and that people benefit from what I say. I experience a feeling of warmth and friendship flowing from the audience towards me. I know that they appreciate my delivery and that they will use my teachings to improve their lives and that makes me happy.

Each day is important to me and what I share of value is rewarded by my audience as they attentively take notes and share their testimonials which are a motivation to continue doing what I am doing. I enjoy a very fulfilling life as a speaker sharing all I have to share with the world."

THE MAGICAL MOUNTAINS RELAXATION SCRIPT

"I imagine myself lying on the grass under a tree on a beautiful autumn day. The sun seeps through the leaves of the tree and there is a cool breeze gently caressing my body keeping me cool.

There are flowers all around me and I relax and my mind unwinds to the sound of the trees above me.

I can hear people enjoying the day in the distance and that makes me happy. I remind myself to relax my body from head to toes. I lay on the fresh green grass and can smell the fragrance of the flowers around me.

There is a fountain with running water, I can hear that too. The water in the fountain is pure, clean, cool and refreshing, and I can hear the birds in the trees chirping away happily. Everything makes me happy and relaxed on this beautiful autumn day.

There is an easy breeze blowing over me and I continue feeling more comfortable and at ease, I can see the flowers moving gently in the breeze, I can smell the fragrance of the flowers... and now I am ready to release and relax..."

HOW TO PUT A GOAL IN YOUR FUTURE

In putting a goal in the future we will travel above the timeline.

We will first think of a goal or something we want happening in the future and make an image of it, give it submodalities, make it an internal representation of that goal. Then travel above your timeline and into the future and trust your unconscious mind to let you know exactly when to drop the internal representation in your future at the right time on the timeline happy and grateful knowing that THE UNIVERSE IS DELIVERING.

ADVANCED – MASTER PRACTITIONER LEVEL NLP

CHAPTER 1

TIME TIMELINES AND REALITY

GENERAL FRAME FOR NLP INTERVENTIONS

The easiest way to explain an NLP Coaching Intervention can be expressed as:

Present State + Appropriate Resources = Desired State

When running an Intervention there are many things we need to do in order to ensure the success of the Intervention:

- We gather information about the present state (eye accessing cues, meta-model violations, non-verbal cues, etc…)
- We identify the Client's desired state and assist them in creating a Well-Formed Outcome.
- We contrast the present state and the desired state.
- We discover the Client's internal resources (this can be done through Guided Search).
- We determine our monitoring strategy for ensuring the success of the intervention.
- We assist the client in making the choices and commitments required to achieve their desired goal/state.
- We rigorously test our work over time.

Calibration: Calibration is important!!!

"Calibration is the process of using the senses (seeing, hearing or feeling) to notice specific shifts in a Client's external state, voice tone, posture, gestures that would indicate an internal shift or change." George Faddoul

Future Pacing: Future Pacing is important!!!

"Future Pacing is the process of associating a person into the future where an external cue will trigger an internal response; once the brain has rehearsed this process, the behaviour should automatically be available in that future context." George Faddoul

GATHERING INFORMATION FOR THE INTERVENTION

Here are some questions to assist the Practitioner in gathering information for the NLP Intervention:

Present State Information:

Is there a present unwanted state or behaviour and if so what is it?

If so in which contexts does it occur and what triggers it?

Is there a positive function behind this state/behaviour and if so will it need to be preserved?

Desired State Information:

What is the Client's Outcome, as in, what new state/behaviour do they want?

Is the Outcome Well Formed (Well Formed Conditions)?

Is the Outcome 'Ecological', is it worth having, what would having it do for the Client?

How will the Client know when they have achieved their Outcome? (Evidence)

Where, when and with whom do they want their Outcome? (Context)

MAJOR NLP PRESUPPOSITIONS

In NLP, as seen before, there are what we call 'Major NLP Presuppositions'.

It can be said that these presuppositions are the pillars of NLP.

Let's have a quick look at them:

- Each person has a unique perception of the world.
- Each person makes the best choice available to them at the time they make it.
- People work perfectly.
- Everything is feedback.
- Every behaviour of yours (and others) has a positive intention.
- The meaning of communication is it's effect (is the result you get).
- There is a solution to every problem.
- We have all the resources within us.
- The 'Map' is not the Territory.
- He who has the greatest flexibility has the greatest influence.
- Mind and Body are one.
- Excellence can be duplicated.
- What we see in others, is true about ourselves (If you spot it, you probably have it).
- Knowledge, thought, memory and imagination are the result of sequences and combinations of ways of filtering and storing information.
- Experience is the best teacher. We learn NLP, not by theoretical study, but by experiencing it.

NEUROLOGICAL LEVELS OF CHANGE

In his book "Changing Belief Systems with NLP". Robert Dilts' Neurological Level Alignment identifies six different levels of experience corresponding to six different levels of neurological 'circuitry'.

Transcendent/Spiritual

At this level the question we need to ask is 'Who else?'

We need to go beyond the self, sense of oneness…

Disconnectedness and aloneness happen at this level.

Re-imprinting can be used at this level amongst other techniques.

Identity

At this level the question we need to ask is 'Who am I?'

At this level we deal with boundaries and establishing healthy boundaries.

At this level we deal with the kind of person we are…

Worthlessness happens at this level.

Re-imprinting, Conflict Integration and Part Re-sequencing can be used at this level amongst other techniques.

Beliefs and Values

At this level the question we need to ask is 'Why?'

At this level we deal with Values, Beliefs and Belief systems, with Causes and Meaning…,

Hopelessness happens at this level.

Re-imprinting and Conflict Integration can be used at this level amongst other techniques.

Capabilities

At this level the question we need to ask is 'How?'

At this level we deal with Strategies, States and Meta-Programs

Helplessness and insecurity happens at this level...

Strategies and Modelling techniques are what we use at this level.

Behaviour

At this level we ask the question 'What?'

At this level we deal with specific things we do, behaviour...

Specific behaviours here are important.

Re-framing and V/K Dissociation techniques are what we use at this level.

Environment

At this level the questions we ask are 'Where' and 'When?

Techniques that focus on Anchoring, Habit's and Rituals are what we use at this level.

OUTCOMES - WELL-FORMED CONDITIONS / KEYS TO AN ACHIEVABLE OUTCOME

In order for anyone to have an achievable outcome they would have to ask themselves a series of questions. (Also the Practitioner can ask the Client these questions.)

In this case let's pretend it is you who wants to plan for an achievable outcome. Following are the questions you would need to ask yourself:

- **'What do I want but don't yet have?'**
  Ask yourself this question at least 3 times until you actually get beyond the superficial answers that don't really mean too much but answer to more superficial needs and wants.

- **'What stops me from having my outcome right now? Or 'Why is it that I don't already have it?'**
- **'Is there more than one way of achieving my outcome?'**
- **'Is there any other way I can achieve the same or similar results with a different outcome?'**
  If your answer is yes then consider other outcomes

- **Make sure once you have the outcome that you set your INTENTION for achieving it.**

- **State what you want/ the outcome you want in the positive (What you do want, not what you don't want)**
- **Ask yourself then 'Is the first step to achieving my outcome specific and achievable ?**
- **Ask yourself 'Can it be initiated by me?' 'Can it be maintained by me?' 'Can it be controlled by me?'**
- **Also notice if what you have is a large global outcome (heal the world) or if it is of a reasonably manageable chunk size? (heal the world, one person at a time)**
  (Chunk down into smaller outcomes if necessesary.)

- **You will be monitoring your progression so next think about the evidence you will require to let you know when you've achieved your outcome. (Remember that all evidence needs to be sensory based: what you see, hear, feel, smell, taste.)**
- **Define the 'Where', 'When', and 'With Who' you want it.**
  (This is what we would call the context of your outcome.)

- **You also need to decide what time-frames are involved?**
- **You are results driven so also ask yourself 'What will achieving this outcome do for me?'**
- **Ask yourself 'What are the positive and negative consequences of getting my outcome?'**
- **Ask yourself 'Is my outcome ecological?' (Good for Self, Others and System or Environment) – If not then it needs to be so might as well rethink your outcome altogether and start over.**
- **Ask yourself then 'What resources do I need to achieve my outcome?'**
- **Ask yourself then 'What resources do I already have to achieve my outcome?'**
- **Ask yourself then 'What other resources do I still need to achieve my outcome?**
  (Some resource examples: Information, attitude, internal state, training, money, help or support from others, etc.)

- **Ask yourself then 'Have I ever had or done this or something similar before?'**
- **Ask yourself then 'Do I know anyone who has?'**
- **Ask yourself then 'Can I act as if I have already achieved my outcome?'**
- **Ask yourself then 'Is the first step to achieving my outcome specific and achievable?**
- **Ask yourself 'What am I already doing to begin to achieve my outcome?'**
- **You might also want to do some FUTURE PACING and Imagine stepping into the future and having your outcome fully. Look back and determine what steps were required to achieve the outcome now that you have it. ('AS-IF Frame')**

Of course if you are an NLP Practitioner or Master Practitioner this is how you would want to guide your Client so follow the steps provided to aid you in assisting your Client.

SUBMODALITY DISTINCTIONS, DRIVERS AND CALIBRATION

The Six Modalities of Calibration are: Visual, Auditory, Kinaesthetic, Olfatory, Gustatory and Auditory Digital.

Just to clarify, 'Modality' refers to our Internal Representations; the Six Modalities of Calibration are the Five Senses or Modalities: Visual, Auditory, Kinaesthetic, Olfactory, and Gustatory PLUS our Internal Dialogue.

Submodalities are the qualities of our experiences.

In NLP, Calibration is known as the skill of learning to read unconscious, non-verbal responses and developing high-level NLP communication skills and techniques using the senses (seeing, hearing or feeling) to notice shifts in a person's external state, voice, posture, gestures, that would indicate an internal shift or change.

Calibration, depends on refined Sensory Acuity; and it is the ability to notice and measure changes with respect to a standard, usually involving the comparison between two different sets of external, non-verbal cues and in this way, by comparing, we notice the difference between person's, places, things, states and behaviours.

Exercise

Following is a listing of our Visual, Auditory and Kinaesthetic Submodalities and Submodality Distinctions.

Think of a pleasant experience and on the right write down its submodality distinctions.

Visual Submodality Distinctions	
Colour/Black and White	
Brightness (Brightness/Dimness)	
Contrast	
Focus	
Texture	
Detail	

Size	
Distance	
Shape	
Border	
Location (Where it originates)	
Orientation	
Movement within the image	
Movement of the image	
Associated/Dissociated	
Perspective	
Proportion	
Dimension (Including Magnification)	
Singular/Plural	
Three other interesting Submodalities are:	
Self/Context (Sometimes a person will see themselves different in a context than a situation is.	
Transparent or not transparent	
Direction of lighting	

Auditory Submodality Distinctions	
Location (Where it originates: A Sound can be of an External or Internal Source. The Direction of an External sound could be coming from: From N, S, E, W, or From Above, Below, the Right, the Left) Hearing Angle/perspective/point of view/ angle from which you hear it, positioning in relation to a particular object (in this case it could be a person or a loud speaker or it could be a noisy footpath or the sound of a school group enjoying a day at the local pools.) The Direction of an Internal sound comes from me, it is Mine in the form of Critical Voices, Commentary Voices, Internal Dialogue.	
Pitch	
Tonality	
Melody	
Inflection	
Volume	
Tempo	
Rhythm	
Duration	
Mono/Stereo	
Another interesting Submodality is: **Resonance with context**	

Kinaesthetic Submodality Distinctions	
Quality	
Intensity	
Location (Where it originates)	
Movement	
Direction	
Speed	
Duration	

NOTE: emotions (meta-feelings) occur as a result of visual, auditory or direct in-put kinaesthetics, but are not actual submodalities.

Our Submodality Distinctions play out a role in our lives, following are two Case Scenarios in which we notice how much they do so.

Case Scenario 1. – SELF IN CONTEXT - WEIGHT LOSS SUCCESS STORY

Example - One of my NLP Trainers, Tim Hallbom worked with a client whose outcome was to lose weight; this client was a woman who wanted to get to her ideal weight for herself but was realizing that she could only get to about 2k from the weight she had as goal.

He noticed that she also had made the comment: 'Who am I to outshine the rest of my family?', so he asked her to look at herself in the context of her family and she was seeing herself as dimmer than the rest of the members of her family (in her mind's eye); this was because she couldn't outshine them.

Tim did a very simple intervention with her asking her to brighten herself up and so she made herself just a little brighter than the rest of her family and the 2k just disappeared basically. (self in the context.- thinking of yourself differently...sometimes we just need to think of ourselves differently but in a more positive light.)

This client visualised herself as less bright in the family system but some people will visualise themselves as not really existing somehow in the family system. Some people visualise themselves as bigger than every other member … (**Self/Context - Sometimes a person will see themselves different in a context than the situation is.**)

Exercise:

Think of an example of your own and try brightening yourself up in their presence and see what happens.

Case Scenario 2. – THE HARMFUL EFFECT OF A LIMITING BELIEF – CANCER PATIENT

In a conversation Tim Hallbom had with another of his clients, a Chinese guy who had cancer, Tim discovers that this client always felt the pressure of his family behind him watching him all the time. Tim notices that this particular client also mentions he is the oldest and therefore also the first born and explains to Tim that the first born in a Chinese family has a special role… (I think they are expected to succeed and somehow be a role model/mentor for the rest of the children/brothers and sisters…). As it turns out, Tim discovers that he isn't actually the first born since he had a brother born before him who had died when they were children, making him the second born…but he saw his family watching him all the time, so that's the sense of self in context, sometimes those things can make such a huge difference to a person's life and well-being…It's like he wasn't in the right place for himself. So sometimes you will find that those kinds of things exist and the way you are represented makes a huge difference in your experience of life. This is a case of what in NLP we call a 'limiting belief' affecting the life experience of someone. Limiting Beliefs are formed in the early stages of psycho-social development.) Was the cancer a result of this limiting belief???…

Do you have Limiting Beliefs about yourself that affect your life experiences???

Exercise:

See if you can find one limiting belief about yourself and think about how you can change your thinking, how you can change your beliefs about yourself to positively affect the way in which you experience life and to prevent any possible ailments that may come as a consequence of having the limiting belief.

EXPLORING SUBMODALITIES

Location is one of many submodalities that makes the quality of our experiences more or less intense. Following we will explore submodalities.

As seen previously in the Submodality Listing, Submodalities in NLP are fine distinctions or the subsets of the Modalities that are part of each representational system that encode and give meaning to our experiences. They are the building blocks of the representational systems by which we code, order and give meaning to the experiences we have. Submodalities are how we structure our experiences.

How do we know what we believe and what we do not believe? We code the two different kinds of beliefs in different Submodalities. We create meaning by using different Submodalities to code our experience, for example someone we like and someone we dislike.

SUBMODALITIES EXPLORATION (Trying on submodalities, Finding Submodality Drivers, Noticing how Intensity of Feeling changes with Submodality Work, and Usefulness of Submodality Change in an Intervention.)

Exercise:

With the purpose of exploring submodality distinctions, and discovering what happens to our experience when we shift submodalities, and to find commonalities think of a pleasant experience and notice how the experience is represented.

Then choose/name a submodality distinction and try it on the experience. (It is important that we only change one submodality at a time and that we return the experience to how it was originally remembered before going on to the next submodality as we do not want to modify anything permanently at this stage.)

After doing this consider if other submodalities shift when using a particular submodality (for instance when using the submodality 'location', do other submodalities such as clarity and brightness change with it?, and if so, then, the submodality we chose to try on, that lead to other submodality shifts is a submodality of a special kind, it is what we call a **'Submodality Driver'** (Also known as a **Critical Submodality**) and they are **'the difference that makes a difference'**. These Submodality Drivers, when changed, will change other Submodalities automatically.

Also consider if the quality or intensity of feelings changes with submodality work.

And then consider in what context this submodality change would be useful in an intervention.

Use the following table to record your experience for each submodality change. (Every time you change a submodality use a new table.)

Experience No.___			
	CHOOSE A SUBMODALITY TO CHANGE AND THEN ENTER THE INFORMATION FOR THE REST OF THE MODALITIES/ SUBMODALITIES REMEMBER TO CHANGE THE SUBMODALITY YOU CHOSE TO CHANGE BACK TO IT'S ORIGINAL SETTINGS	REPORT ON WHETHER THERE HAVE BEEN CHANGES TO OTHER SUBMODALITIES WITH A 'YES' OR A 'NO' IN EACH ROW FOR ALL THREE MODALITIES	WAS THE SUBMODALITY YOU CHOSE TO CHANGE A DRIVER? ANSWER WITH THE WORD 'DRIVER' IF SO IN THE SUBMODALITY'S ROW BELOW
VISUAL REPRESENTATIONAL SYSTEM/MODALITY **WHAT DO YOU SEE?** **Visual Submodality Distinctions** **IN THIS COLUME describe your experience making use of the following questions to elicit Visual Submodality Distinctions**			
Colour/Black and White **Is it in colour or in black and white?** **Is it full colour spectrum?** **Are the colours vivid or washed out?**			
Brightness (Brightness/Dimness) **In that context, is it brighter or darker/dimmer than normal?**			
Contrast **Is it high contrast (vivid) or washed out?**			

Focus **Is the image sharp in focus or is it fuzzy?**			
Texture **Is the image smooth or rough textured?**			
Detail **Are there foreground and background details?** **Do you see the details as part of a whole or do you have to shift focus to see them?**			
Size **How big is the picture (Specific Estimated Size in inches (ex. 11"x14")**			
Distance **How far away is the image?**			
Shape **What shape is the picture: square, rectangle, round?**			
Border **Is there a border around it or do the edges fuzz out?** **Does the border have a colour?** **How thick is the border?**			
Location (Where it originates) **Where is the image located in space?** **Show me with both hands where you see the image/s.**			

Orientation **Is the image portrait or landscape?** **Is the picture tilted?**			
Movement within the image **Is it a movie or a still picture?** **How rapid is the movement: faster or slower than normal?**			
Movement of the image **Is the image stable?** **What direction does it move/spin in?** **How fast is it moving: fast, moderate, slow?**			
Associated/Dissociated **Do you see yourself or do you see the event as if you were there?**			
Perspective **From what perspective do you see it?** **If dissociated, do you see yourself from the right, left, back or front?**			
Proportion **Are the people and things in the image in proportion to one another and to yourself or are some of them larger or smaller than life? (self in context – see below)**			
Dimension (Including Magnification) **Is it flat or is it three-dimensional? 2D or 3D ?** **Does the picture wrap around you?**			

Singular/Plural **Is there one image or more than one?** **Do you see them one after the other or at the same time?**			
3 OTHER INTERESTING SUBMODALITIES ARE:			
SELF IN CONTEXT (Sometimes a person will see themselves different in a context than a situation is. **Perception of Self in Context? (Ex. Seeing yourself brighter or dimmer than everyone else)**			
TRANSPARENT OR NOT TRANSPARENT **Is the image transparent or not?**			
DIRECTION OF LIGHTING **What direction is the lighting coming from?**			
AUDITORY REPRESENTATIONAL SYSTEM/ MODALITY **WHAT DO YOU HEAR?** **ARE THERE ANY SOUNDS THAT ARE IMPORTANT?** **Auditory Submodality Distinctions** **Continue IN THIS COLUME and describe your experience making use of the following Questions to elicit Auditory Submodality Distinctions**			

Location/Where it originates: A Sound can be of an External or Internal Source. **Is the sound or voice internal or external?** The Direction of an External sound could be coming from: From N, S, E, W, or From Above, Below, the Right, the Left) **If the sound or voice is external where is it coming from: N, S , E, W/ Above, Below, Left, Right??** Hearing Angle/perspective/point of view/angle from which you hear it, positioning in relation to a particular object (in this case it could be a person or a loud speaker or it could be a noisy footpath or the sound of a school group enjoying a day at the local pools.) **Where is it coming from your point of view/angle from which you hear it, positioning in relation to a particular object?** The Direction of an Internal sound comes from me, it is Mine in the form of Critical Voices, Commentary Voices, Internal Dialogue. **If the voice or sound is internal, is it in the form of Critical Voices, Commentary Voices, or Internal Dialogue?**			
Pitch **Is it high-pitched or low-pitched?** **Is the pitch higher or lower than normal?**			

Tonality **What is the tonality: nasal, full and rich, thin, grating?**			
Melody **Is it a monotone or is there a melodic range?**			
Inflection **Which parts are accentuated?**			
Volume **How loud is it?**			
Tempo **Is it fast or slow?**			
Rhythm **Does it have a beat or a cadence?**			
Duration **Is it continuous or intermittent?**			
Mono/Stereo **Do you hear it on one side, both sides, or is the sound all around you?**			
Another interesting Submodality is: **Resonance with context** **Does the voice or sound Resonate with the Context?**			
KINAESTHETIC REPRESENTATIONAL SYSTEM/ MODALITY **WHAT DO YOU FEEL?** **ARE THERE ANY FEELINGS THAT ARE IMPORTANT?** **Kinaesthetic Submodality Distinctions** **Continue IN THIS COLUME and describe your experience making use of the following Questions to elicit Kinaesthetic Submodality Distinctions**			

Quality **How would you describe the body sensation: tingling, warm, cold, relaxed, tense, knotted, diffused?**			
Intensity **How strong is the sensation? (From 1 to 10)**			
Location (Where it originates) **Where do you feel it in your body? (Face, upper body, lower body, extremities…etc)**			
Movement **Is there movement in the sensation?** **Is the movement continuous or does it come in waves?**			
Direction **Where does the sensation start?** **How does it get from the place of origin to the place where you are most aware of it?**			
Speed **Is it a slow steady progression or does it move in a rush?**			
Duration **Is it continuous or intermittent?**			

Changing Submodalities is a very effective and powerful way of changing the meaning of an experience.

THE POWER OF SUBMODALITY WORK TO DESIGN OUR FUTURE

In NLP, we can do Submodality Work when we are setting a goal, and the more attention we pay to the Submodalities, the more specifically refined our goal becomes. We need to remember that the finer our distinctions, the more clearly and creatively we can design our future.

BRINGING WHAT WE LIKE CLOSER AND TAKING WHAT WE DISLIKE FURTHER AWAY

Are the pictures you make affecting you? YES THEY ARE

When setting goals it is important to make sure we bring the picture as close as possible to us making it bigger, brighter, clearer, louder; this will make us feel closer to it also and it will feel more likely for us to achieve it.

Choosing to take a negative picture further away will automatically release the focus we have on it and it's effect will seem to dissipate.

Exercise:

Think of a goal and ask yourself if you are 'seeing a picture' and ask yourself whether it would make any difference if the picture was placed closer or further from you.

Experiment taking it further away and bringing it closer to you and write down your findings.

SUBMODALITY WORK - MAKING SOMETHING MORE OR LESS LIKABLE

Making something more or less likable is all about changing that 'thing's' submodalities… Location can be a big changer…

1. Think about something you dislike. Call it A. Point to where it is, where you see it. Think about what submodalities describe it?
2. Think about something you like. Call it B. Point to where it is, where you see it. What submodalities describe it?
3. HOW TO LIKE SOMETHING THAT YOU DISLIKE AT PRESENT - Take A waaaaay out far and away from you and bring it back to where you saw B (making sure to apply all the submodalities you found described B).
4. How does it feel? Is it good for you? If it is leave it there, if it isn't then take it back to how it was before.

5. HOW TO DISLIKE SOMETHING THAT YOU LIKE AT PRESENT - Take B waaaay out far and away from you and bring it back to where you saw A (making sure to apply all the submodalities you found described A).

6. How does it feel? Is it good for you? If it is leave it there, if it isn't then take it back to how it was before.
    SUBMODALITY WORK GIVES YOU A LOT MORE CHOICE OVER YOUR EXPERIENCES.

You might find it useful to use a Submodality Checklist

SUBMODALITY CHECKLIST – WHAT DO YOU SEE, HEAR, FEEL?

	WHAT YOU LIKE	WHAT YOU DISLIKE
VISUAL REPRESENTATIONAL SYSTEM/MODALITY **WHAT DO YOU SEE?** **Visual Submodality Distinctions** **IN THIS COLUME describe your experience making use of the following questions to elicit Visual Submodality Distinctions**		
Colour/Black and White **Is it in colour or in black and white?** **Is it full colour spectrum?** **Are the colours vivid or washed out?**		
Brightness (Brightness/Dimness) **In that context, is it brighter or darker/ dimmer than normal?**		
Contrast **Is it high contrast (vivid) or washed out?**		
Focus **Is the image sharp in focus or is it fuzzy?**		
Texture **Is the image smooth or rough textured?**		

Detail **Are there foreground and background details?** **Do you see the details as part of a whole or do you have to shift focus to see them?**		
Size **How big is the picture (Specific Estimated Size in inches (ex. 11"x14")**		
Distance **How far away is the image?**		
Shape **What shape is the picture: square, rectangle, round?**		
Border **Is there a border around it or do the edges fuzz out?** **Does the border have a colour?** **How thick is the border?**		
Location (Where it originates) **Where is the image located in space?** **Show me with both hands where you see the image/s.**		
Orientation **Is the image portrait or landscape?** **Is the picture tilted?**		

Movement within the image **Is it a movie or a still picture?** **How rapid is the movement: faster or slower than normal?**		
Movement of the image **Is the image stable?** **What direction does it move/spin in?** **How fast is it moving: fast, moderate, slow?**		
Associated/Dissociated **Do you see yourself or do you see the event as if you were there?**		
Perspective **From what perspective do you see it?** **If dissociated, do you see yourself from the right, left, back or front?**		
Proportion **Are the people and things in the image in proportion to one another and to yourself or are some of them larger or smaller than life? (self in context – see below)**		
Dimension (Including Magnification) **Is it flat or is it three-dimensional? 2D or 3D?** **Does the picture wrap around you?**		

Singular/Plural **Is there one image or more than one?** **Do you see them one after the other or at the same time?**		
3 OTHER INTERESTING SUBMODALITIES ARE:		
SELF IN CONTEXT (Sometimes a person will see themselves different in a context than a situation is. **Perception of Self in Context? (Ex. Seeing yourself brighter or dimmer than everyone else)**		
TRANSPARENT OR NOT TRANSPARENT **Is the image transparent or not?**		
DIRECTION OF LIGHTING **What direction is the lighting coming from?**		
AUDITORY REPRESENTATIONAL SYSTEM/MODALITY **WHAT DO YOU HEAR?** **ARE THERE ANY SOUNDS THAT ARE IMPORTANT?** **Auditory Submodality Distinctions** **Continue IN THIS COLUME and describe your experience making use of the following Questions to elicit Auditory Submodality Distinctions**		

Location/Where it originates: A Sound can be of an External or Internal Source. **Is the sound or voice internal or external?** The Direction of an External sound could be coming from: From N, S, E, W, or From Above, Below, the Right, the Left) **If the sound or voice is external where is it coming from: N, S, E, W/Above, Below, Left, Right??** Hearing Angle/perspective/point of view/ angle from which you hear it, positioning in relation to a particular object (in this case it could be a person or a loud speaker or it could be a noisy footpath or the sound of a school group enjoying a day at the local pools.) **Where is it coming from your point of view/angle from which you hear it, positioning in relation to a particular object?** The Direction of an Internal sound comes from me, it is Mine in the form of Critical Voices, Commentary Voices, Internal Dialogue. **If the voice or sound is internal, is it in the form of Critical Voices, Commentary Voices, or Internal Dialogue?**		
Pitch **Is it high-pitched or low-pitched?** **Is the pitch higher or lower than normal?**		
Tonality **What is the tonality: nasal, full and rich, thin, grating?**		

Melody **Is it a monotone or is there a melodic range?**		
Inflection **Which parts are accentuated?**		
Volume **How loud is it?**		
Tempo **Is it fast or slow?**		
Rhythm **Does it have a beat or a cadence?**		
Duration **Is it continuous or intermittent?**		
Mono/Stereo **Do you hear it on one side, both sides, or is the sound all around you?**		
Another interesting Submodality is: **Resonance with context** **Does the voice or sound Resonate with the Context?**		
KINAESTHETIC REPRESENTATIONAL SYSTEM/ MODALITY **WHAT DO YOU FEEL?** **ARE THERE ANY FEELINGS THAT ARE IMPORTANT?** **Kinaesthetic Submodality Distinctions** **Continue IN THIS COLUME and describe your experience making use of the following Questions to elicit Kinaesthetic Submodality Distinctions**		
Quality **How would you describe the body sensation: tingling, warm, cold, relaxed, tense, knotted, diffused?**		

Intensity **How strong is the sensation? (From 1 to 10)**		
Location (Where it originates) **Where do you feel it in your body? (Face, upper body, lower body, extremities…etc)**		
Movement **Is there movement in the sensation?** **Is the movement continuous or does it come in waves?**		
Direction **Where does the sensation start?** **How does it get from the place of origin to the place where you are most aware of it?**		
Speed **Is it a slow steady progression or does it move in a rush?**		
Duration **Is it continuous or intermittent?**		

IDENTIFYING SUBMODALITY ACCESSING CUES (READING PHYSIOLOGY)

In NLP, Submodality Accessing Cues are unconscious behaviours; these behaviours are: breathing, gestures, posture, head movements and the eye movements that indicate which specific sensory modality or representational system is being used to process/think of information internally (visual auditory or kinaesthetic.

It is important to consider whether the person we are observing is remembering or creating and whether the person is displaying signs of internal dialogue. (Refer to eye accessing cues covered in the NLP Practitioner Training section of this book.)

The purpose of Submodality Accessing Cues is to begin to read shifts in physiology depending on submodality distinctions and to discover commonalities (what in our experience is common to everyone).

READING SUBMODALITY ACCESSING CUES TO DETERMINE SUBMODALITY DISTINCTIONS BEING USED IN SUBMODALITY WORK

You need at least two people for this exercise:

With the purpose of beginning to read physiology depending on submodality distinctions and to discover commonalities two people find a picture that is emotionally neutral and choose a submodality to vary in both experiences. Then both will compare similarities in Accessing Cues.

Reminder: Accessing Cues are unconscious behaviours, including breathing, gestures, posture, head movements and eye movements that indicate which specific sensory modality or representational system is being used to process/think of information internally.

Use the following table:

Experience No.__		
	CHOOSE A SUBMODALITY TO CHANGE AND THEN ENTER THE INFORMATION FOR THE REST OF THE MODALITIES/ SUBMODALITIES REMEMBER TO CHANGE THE SUBMODALITY YOU CHOSE TO CHANGE BACK TO IT'S ORIGINAL SETTINGS	REPORT ON ACCESSING CUES
VISUAL REPRESENTATIONAL SYSTEM/ MODALITY **WHAT DO YOU SEE?** **Visual Submodality Distinctions** **IN THIS COLUME describe your experience making use of the following questions to elicit Visual Submodality Distinctions**		
Colour/Black and White **Is it in colour or in black and white?** **Is it full colour spectrum?** **Are the colours vivid or washed out?**		
Brightness (Brightness/Dimness) **In that context, is it brighter or darker/dimmer than normal?**		

Contrast **Is it high contrast (vivid) or washed out?**		
Focus **Is the image sharp in focus or is it fuzzy?**		
Texture **Is the image smooth or rough textured?**		
Detail **Are there foreground and background details?** **Do you see the details as part of a whole or do you have to shift focus to see them?**		
Size **How big is the picture (Specific Estimated Size in inches (ex. 11"x14")**		
Distance **How far away is the image?**		
Shape **What shape is the picture: square, rectangle, round?**		
Border **Is there a border around it or do the edges fuzz out?** **Does the border have a colour?** **How thick is the border?**		

Location (Where it originates) **Where is the image located in space?** **Show me with both hands where you see the image/s.**		
Orientation **Is the image portrait or landscape?** **Is the picture tilted?**		
Movement within the image **Is it a movie or a still picture?** **How rapid is the movement: faster or slower than normal?**		
Movement of the image **Is the image stable?** **What direction does it move/spin in?** **How fast is it moving: fast, moderate, slow?**		
Associated/Dissociated **Do you see yourself or do you see the event as if you were there?**		
Perspective **From what perspective do you see it?** **If dissociated, do you see yourself from the right, left, back or front?**		
Proportion **Are the people and things in the image in proportion to one another and to yourself or are some of them larger or smaller than life? (self in context – see below)**		

Dimension (Including Magnification) **Is it flat or is it three-dimensional? 2D or 3D?** **Does the picture wrap around you?**		
Singular/Plural **Is there one image or more than one?** **Do you see them one after the other or at the same time?**		
3 OTHER INTERESTING SUBMODALITIES ARE:		
SELF IN CONTEXT (Sometimes a person will see themselves different in a context than a situation is. **Perception of Self in Context? (Ex. Seeing yourself brighter or dimmer than everyone else)**		
TRANSPARENT OR NOT TRANSPARENT **Is the image transparent or not?**		
DIRECTION OF LIGHTING **What direction is the lighting coming from?**		
AUDITORY REPRESENTATIONAL SYSTEM/ MODALITY **WHAT DO YOU HEAR?** **ARE THERE ANY SOUNDS THAT ARE IMPORTANT?** **Auditory Submodality Distinctions** **Continue IN THIS COLUME and describe your experience making use of the following Questions to elicit Auditory Submodality Distinctions**		

Location/Where it originates: A Sound can be of an External or Internal Source. **Is the sound or voice internal or external?** The Direction of an External sound could be coming from: From N, S, E, W, or From Above, Below, the Right, the Left) **If the sound or voice is external where is it coming from: N, S, E, W/Above, Below, Left, Right??** Hearing Angle/perspective/point of view/angle from which you hear it, positioning in relation to a particular object (in this case it could be a person or a loud speaker or it could be a noisy footpath or the sound of a school group enjoying a day at the local pools.) **Where is it coming from your point of view/angle from which you hear it, positioning in relation to a particular object?** The Direction of an Internal sound comes from me, it is Mine in the form of Critical Voices, Commentary Voices, Internal Dialogue. **If the voice or sound is internal, is it in the form of Critical Voices, Commentary Voices, or Internal Dialogue?**		
Pitch **Is it high-pitched or low-pitched?** **Is the pitch higher or lower than normal?**		
Tonality **What is the tonality: nasal, full and rich, thin, grating?**		
Melody **Is it a monotone or is there a melodic range?**		
Inflection **Which parts are accentuated?**		

Volume **How loud is it?**		
Tempo **Is it fast or slow?**		
Rhythm **Does it have a beat or a cadence?**		
Duration **Is it continuous or intermittent?**		
Mono/Stereo **Do you hear it on one side, both sides, or is the sound all around you?**		
Another interesting Submodality is: **Resonance with context** **Does the voice or sound Resonate with the Context?**		
KINAESTHETIC REPRESENTATIONAL SYSTEM/MODALITY **WHAT DO YOU FEEL?** **ARE THERE ANY FEELINGS THAT ARE IMPORTANT?** **Kinaesthetic Submodality Distinctions** **Continue IN THIS COLUME and describe your experience making use of the following Questions to elicit Kinaesthetic Submodality Distinctions**		
Quality **How would you describe the body sensation: tingling, warm, cold, relaxed, tense, knotted, diffused?**		
Intensity **How strong is the sensation? (From 1 to 10)**		

Location (Where it originates) **Where do you feel it in your body? (Face, upper body, lower body, extremities...etc)**		
Movement **Is there movement in the sensation?** **Is the movement continuous or does it come in waves?**		
Direction **Where does the sensation start?** **How does it get from the place of origin to the place where you are most aware of it?**		
Speed **Is it a slow steady progression or does it move in a rush?**		
Duration **Is it continuous or intermittent?**		

As we have seen, submodalities play an important role in assisting us in identifying the structure of subjective experience.

We have learnt how to calibrate what someone is doing on the inside.

We have learnt that we all experience things differently.

SUBMODALITIES OF TIME

We all make Time Distinctions. People's Internal Timelines orient them differently in terms of Past, Present, and Future. We can all learn how to utilise Time when creating change for ourselves and others.

The purpose of Submodalities of Time is to determine how a person makes time distinctions, how internal time lines may orient people differently in terms of past, present and future and how to utilise time when creating change for self and others.

The following exercise will show us how a person makes time distinctions, it will show us how our internal Timelines orient us differently in terms of Past, Present and Future and will teach us how to utilise Time when creating change for ourselves and others.

In groups of 2 do the following:

1. Elicit submodalities of time by asking your partner to identify some emotionally neutral activity that he or she does every day, such as brushing their teeth, combing their hair, etc. Ask the person to imagine/represent in their mind's eye doing the activity today, yesterday, last week, a month ago, a year ago, five years ago.
2. Then ask them to represent doing the activity in the future making use of the same time increments.
3. Use submodalities such as LOCATION, COLOUR/BLACK AND WHITE, ASSOCIATED/DISASSOCIATED, SIZE, BRIGHTNESS AND CLARITY to explore.
4. Float above your timeline and notice what it looks like from that dissociated perspective. Be sure to reassociate.

Notice that for most people Time will be organised in a linear way.

We all have a way of organising Time, some people have ways of organising time that actually serves them well some have ways that don't. The way we organise time needs to be tailored to our own way of thinking.

There is a lot we can do with our timelines:

1. FIND OUT THE STRUCTURE OF THE TIMELINE - To find out how you organise time (identifying your timeline)
2. CHANGE THE TIMELINE - To change the way you organise time if it's not really serving you by changing the timeline
3. USE THE TIMELINE TO ADDRESS PROBLEMS - You can make changes on the timeline – addressing problem memories that come up from time to time, clear feelings, reorganise thinking, take another look at events that we gave meaning etc…
4. CREATING A COMPELLING FUTURE

CREATING A COMPELLING FUTURE – In general for most people it's going to be better to have a compelling future than a compelling past. Think about what you would like to experience in the future, it's all about this. Planning for the future is important - Financial Planning, Planning for Retirement…. Once you have a target you can start moving towards it and you can start modifying your behaviour to get there.

Predicting has so much to do with organising time.

In NLP we say "Timelines are coded at an unconscious level but we can make the unconscious conscious by drawing our timeline and by physicalising it so we can work with it."

We can also try on other people's timeline and see what shifts in our experience as we are all so different and therefore we have different experiences to the same events, we all experience the same events differently.

Once we organise time we can pretty much start predicting what's going to happen in the future.

There is an exercises that anyone can do and it is all about picking a goal and turning it into a movie of what it would be like to have achieved the goal and the more specific you make it the better so you could ask yourself what you see hear and feel and make it as real as possible. You could also ask yourself what you are thinking at the time.

CREATING A COMPELLING FUTURE THAT SETS A POSITIVE DIRECTION

Another exercise you could do is to first physicalise your timeline on the floor and as an observer go back 5 years and observe your past and what actions and thoughts brought you to today including the environment, the behaviours, the capabilities and beliefs Consider the environment, behaviours, capabilities and beliefs that were then present and operational throughout the 5 year period leading to 'you' now and how responsible they are of creating the 'you' you are now, today and then project yourself into the future 5 years from now and notice what you'll be like if you continue on your current path without altering your environment, behaviours, capabilities, or beliefs and ask yourself if you will be pleased with the future you and if it is necessary to change the future you and if so and reconsider relationships, health, recreation, career, etc, in other words consider all areas of life as well as life-style habit's, beliefs and above all your thinking (still in the future/working in the future) and write down at least 10 attributes you'd like to have

1_____

2_____

3_____

4_____

5_____

6_____

7_____

8_____

9_____

10_____

SHIFTING AN EXPERIENCE BY CHANGING THE TIMELINE

Changing our timeline gives us a different orientation and can make a shift in our experience.

We can make the conscious decision to stand back and look at it in certain contexts just by setting that intention around it.

Once we've got a timeline, and we know what it is, there is a lot that we can do with it.

Following we will explore submodalities of time and how we organise time in our mind.

EXERCISES FOR SUBMODALITIES OF TIME

Let's explore submodalities of time and, how we organise time in our mind.

(The following four exercises were shared by Tim Hallbom during an NLP Seminar.)

Exercise 1:

Get a sense of your timeline and find some incident or situation that was unpleasant (not your worst – this is just to try it out) someone that was annoyed with you or someone you got annoyed with, something you still have some feelings about, maybe someone that was rude,.

Float above your timeline and float back above that experience so that you are above it about 10 meters up so that you are looking down on it.

Notice what it's like from there and notice that if you drop down towards it you start getting the feelings of it (if you drop down right into it you can get them) so drop right into it and be there again.

Go back up, raise yourself up and before it like you're up and earlier and earlier in time so you're way up and back away from it, higher and higher and the higher you go and it's in front of you notice how your feelings dissipate and at some point the feelings will go away and you won't have much feeling, it will just be an experience out there. You can do this with very powerful feelings like a phobias, if you move back far enough away like this then you can move away from those powerful feelings and it will give you some distance from it.

Exercise 2:

Go back and find a problem you had once that now is just a faded old memory that you resolved a long time ago, that is no big deal anymore (you're in high school, in your twenties or something like that) but now it's way back there it's no big deal and when you get one of those faded ones notice how you feel about it, what are your submodalities like of it. Sometimes just by saying words like 'faded old memories' you'll get ones that are all faded out, it's like it's not a big deal anymore.

Now float back over the one that was a problem that we just moved away from, have a look at it and then move way out into the future, way beyond now way way out until you can look way back in time, way beyond the point of where you resolved whatever this issue is where you had the feelings and look back at it and it's a faded old memory, maybe it's 20 years from now, just look back on it and it's no big deal anymore, you resolved that a long time ago.

Now float back to now and just drop down on your timeline into right here and think back to that situation that gave you some emotion and what's it like now? Is it different? For most people there shouldn't be much feeling tied to it.

Exercise 3:

Think of a problem you had as a child (and again don't choose the worst thing you can think of but choose something that affects you in some way where if you think about it you still get some feelings about it.) Then float up above your timeline and float back to before that event to a couple of weeks before that event, then float down on your timeline being present two weeks before it occurred that is and from that point look through your timeline all the way to now and see who you are now, the kind of person you've become and notice that if you look through life, life is going to have ups and downs and experiences and we'll give meaning to it and if you look all the way through time to now, how does that change that event for you? It puts it in perspective doesn't it? It's just an event that occurred that at the time you might have given it great meaning and anxiety but if you want to start building a lot more trust in yourself and in life float down before a negative and then look through it to now and often that will release the emotions and anxiety of it.

Exercise 4

Stand on your timeline in the present with your future going forward and your past behind you going in the opposite direction. Step on it like you're on the highway of time. So instead of having the timeline however it goes now we're going to just imagine it's like a railroad track and you're standing in the middle of it. Get a sense of being in the here and now and you're fully associated. Anchor the moment with your body. Turn and look at your past as it goes all the way back to birth. Look forward again. Think of the future as being a highway of time, a straight road and really get a sense of that.

Now step away from your timeline and see yourself on the timeline in the present and you can see your future and your past and get that feeling of being a witness of time (you are through-time here).

(If we build a timeline that is physical we make it easier to step in and out of time.)

Now step back onto your timeline in the present with the future ahead of you and the past behind you and experience again what it's like being in-time.

Now move away from your timeline again and look away from it and experience what it feels like to be out-of-time. You will feel like you want to know what's going on. When you are out-of-time or not-in-time you will feel like you are free from it all (like time has stopped and you can do whatever you want or need to do) and it can be a really powerful experience for some people and it gives you the ability to build resources or gather up states that you wouldn't otherwise be able to get when you're time-bound. When you meditate it's really easy to get into meditating by just stepping away from your timeline and leaving it behind like this.

Then go and step back on your timeline and experience the here and now again with all it's submodalities anchoring back into the now. (This is how you end this exercise, making sure you are in the present again on your timeline as you were at the beginning. It is an exercise that allows you to feel the different positions you can adopt with respect to your timeline and how each is different from the others in that our experience is noticeably different.)

PREMATURE COGNITIVE COMMITMENTS

As we go through life from conception on we're encountered with a series of experiences and every one of those experiences we give meaning to in some way; in particular earlier experiences that are novel or unusual are the first ones and the ones with which we build what is called Premature Cognitive Commitments.

We too make these commitments to an environment just like the bee that makes a commitment to a particular window because that was the way out or the fish that is put in an aquarium and partitioned off to one side of the aquarium and once the partition is lifted still continues to swim around in the same space, and the elephant that is as a baby tied to a post with a rope and then grows into an adult and continues to believe that it is tied to the post by a rope that still won't let him move when it can easily break free... We too make Premature Cognitive Commitments and these are perceptual, we put meaning to our experiences and tend to operate from these meanings for the rest of our life.

In the same way anyone who from an early age learns that there are no negative experiences but rather learning experiences will be making a Premature Cognitive Commitment that brings them many learning experiences throughout their life.

LIFE REFRAMING

With Life Reframing we can go back and recreate the meaning that we have in an experience.

We can go back and recreate the meaning that we have in an experience by finding an incident in our life that has lead us to operate in the way you do today and taking a new look at it and reframing it, finding another meaning for it that is valuable and then taking it through our entire lifeline all the way from beginning to end.

ALIGNMENT (APPRECIATION & GRATITUDE, GOALS, INTENT AND BELIEFS)

There are many things which are important when communicating, one of them is to think before we talk and to think positively. Language can direct our attention and the attention of whom we are talking to.

We need to speak positively to ourselves and also to others. We need to make our communication uplifting both when speaking to ourselves as well as in our conversations with others.

One way we direct our attention is with language; the other way we direct our attention is with submodalities so we need to make our future bigger and brighter. What is important to us is what will be driving our attention. Meta-Programs direct attention (some people will sort by what's positive, what's negative, past, present).

Whatever we put our attention on will direct our state of mind.

Different States/States of Mind are going to produce different experiences in life

An example of this is when we're in-love that everything seems beautiful.

Some Resource States are very powerful both psychologically and physiologically.

HeartMath is a research institute that has done a lot of research around the heart and how the heart works and they've made a lot of very important discoveries. They have discovered that the bio-electricity from our hearts is far greater than the bio-electricity from our brains and they now have instruments that can measure it as far out from your body as 3 meters. They have also discovered that different states have different amplitudes of this bio-electricity, so if we are in a certain kind of state of mind, we are in a lot less if we're feeling annoyed and put upon and moody, it pulls our energy way in to the point in which it is almost undetectable.

When people are in States of appreciation and gratitude they can measure it out to about 3 meters.

The states of appreciation and gratitude are the two most powerful states they were able to identify.

They also discovered that if we can get into a State of gratitude and stay there for up to 5 minutes, the physical effects on our immune system lasts up to 6 hours, we have more T Cells and our IGA is much higher, those kinds of things so our immune system improves its functioning.

To succeed and get what you want in life there are four important things to remember to focus on:

- Appreciation and Gratitude are the states of abundance.
- Goals - A goal is about end result
- Intent - intent is about the experience that we're having
- Beliefs – Having empowering beliefs

If all these are in alignment we will tend to get what we want fairly easy.

If we change any one of these they all affect each other, these are all interacting with each other all the time and of course our beliefs are what give us permission to have what we want or not.

LIMITING BELIEFS/LIMITATIONS

In NLP we talk about Limiting beliefs as those which constrain us in some way; just by believing them, we do not think, do or say the things that they inhibit and in doing so we impoverish our lives.

We all have beliefs about rights, duties, abilities, permissions and so on, they are often about ourself and our self-identity but they can also be about other people and the world in general.

It is important to remind ourselves that how we define ourselves and the world around us can be very limiting. We can have all sorts of beliefs of 'how the world works'.

When we identify a limiting belief, in NLP, we put it through Sleight of Mouth…

Lets have a look at Sleight of Mouth/Verb Tenses…

SLEIGHT OF MOUTH / VERB TENSES

Sleight of mouth are a set of linguistic patterns developed by Robert Dilts, they are a series of verbal reframes designed to add flexibility to stuck states and behaviours, they are used to widen a person's perspective and help influence and/or change beliefs so it is important to learn them as part of our NLP training.

We know that when behaviours are programmed they are ordered in a time sequence and that Time distinctions are expressed primarily by verb tenses. To determine how we would represent verb tenses internally we take any simple behaviour and notice how the submodalities shift when the same content shifts position in time via the three simple verb tenses – past present and future.

Even though we are considering them useful, verb tense shifts will rarely be enough in themselves to accomplish a change; if we're doing a swish for instance we need to first elicit the two pictures whether we do it covertly and or conversationally, then the verb shift can be used to link them in time to accomplish the swish transition.

Verb tenses affect experience and there are external nonverbal shifts that indicate that the Client's experience has changed; utilizing them helps create more resourcefulness in any context.

It is important to consider putting 'limits' need in the past and 'resources' in the present and or future, and, we can do this by just changing verb tenses.

Richard Bandler uses verb tense shifts to presuppose that a change has been made and that the old behaviour is now in the past.

We will see more on Sleight of Mouth Patterns further ahead.

Exercise

Try finding a limitation and experimenting with different verb tenses.

META-PROGRAMS

In NLP, Meta-Programs are behavioural schemes deriving from our personal way of selecting possible choices and they are the bases for our decisions.

It has been said that once people believed that each human being was born with a fixed character, steady and unchangeable, and, that each of us had a stable personality that characterised our behaviour making it possible to foresee our future actions. Meta-Programs are only superficially like character, they are more like flexible characteristics changeable using NLP strategies.

Meta-Programs collaborate with other strategies such as VAKOG, beliefs and generalisations to make up our map of the world.

In NLP, the process of identifying Meta-Pprograms is basically that of charting out how different people work differently.

We know that different people have for various reasons different modes of operating, either consistently or in specific situations very often specialising and emphasising one mode of behaviour to the exclusion of others; those modes of behaviour are the Meta-Programs.

Meta-Programs are unconscious, abstract and content free yet very powerful perceptual filters designed to operate across different contexts to create our model of the world helping us determine how we sort and make sense of our world, how we orient to and chunk our experiences and helping us determine what we pay attention to or what to focus our attention on. They are sometimes also called Meta-Sorts.

Although we are all capable of any style of thinking and/or mode of behaviour, we habitually tend to prefer to stay close to one end of the spectrum in each of the Meta-Programs. Neither is right or wrong, only appropriate or inappropriate for particular roles or tasks.

We know we are in rapport with people we perceive as being like us so it's likely we will prefer them to others. These preferred thinking styles are not inflexible, we can all use any of them if we choose to do so, although practice will probably be needed to loosen our deeply embedded habit's.

One of the most valuable goals of personal development is to develop a range of thinking styles and/or modes of behaviour.

The benefit of Meta-Programs is that we tend to achieve rapport with somebody else by approximating their way of thinking and behaving, so, if we can recognise how somebody else works we can translate our position into their language and vice versa, so, we can understand what they say to the degree that they translate their intentions into our language.

If we can recognise differences in how each of us operates and do it without having to judge it, without having to accuse the people different from ourselves of being wrong and being unwilling to see it our way, then we might get along much better.

By seeking to understand and encompass all modes of operation one can become a more whole person, and also be more able to get along with anybody at any time.

This will really start making sense to you when you begin observing these patterns of behaviour in both yourself and others, also when you have an idea of what you want to change about yourself and when you start finding ways to best interact with others based upon your preferred behavioural patterns or Meta-Programs.

There are about fifty known and enlisted Meta-Programs, I will mention some of the more important ones here:

1. Direction: Towards/Away From
2. Source: Internal/External (Self/Others)
3. Options/Procedures
4. Match/Mismatch (Sameness/Difference)
5. Necessity/Possibility
6. Chunk Size: Chunk up/Chunk down
   (General/Specific, Overview/Detail, Big Picture/Small Picture)
7. Stableness/Change
8. Past/Present/Future
9. Active/Passive
10. Proactive/Reactive
11. Environment: Independent/Proximity/Cooperative
12. Rule Structure: My/My
                           My/.:
                           No/My
                           My/Your

13. Convincer:

    Channel: See/Hear/Read/Do
    Mode: No of Times or Examples/ Automatic/Consistent/Period of Time

14. Content Sorts: People/Things/Information/Location

Exercise:

Can you think of an example to the following Meta-Programs.

Direction: Towards/Away From

Some people will move Towards what they want while others will move Away From what they don't want.

Example

....
....
....

Source: Internal/External (Self/Others)

Some people live in perfect happiness and don't give a damn about what people think of them while others are worried about other people's opinions.

Example

....
....
....

Options/Procedures

Some people want lots of choice and develop alternatives while others are good at following set procedures and look for a process that works rather than choices.

Example

....
....
....

Match/Mismatch (Sameness/Difference)

Some people notice similarities in a comparison while other people notice differences in the same comparison.

Example

....
....
....

Necessity/Possibility

Some people look at problems they need solving while others look at possible paths to follow.

Example

....
....
....

Chunk Size: Chunk up/Chunk down

(General/Specific, Overview/Detail, Big Picture/Small Picture)

Some people focus on the big picture while others focus on the detail.

Example

....
....
....

Stableness/Change

Some people might look for a monotonous job while others might look for a challenging and ever-changing position.

Example

....
....
....

Past/Present/Future

Some people live in the past whilst others live in the present and look forward to the future.

Example

....
....
....

Active/Passive

Some people are out there actively seeking opportunities whilst others passively live through events that unfold.

Example

....
....
....

Proactive/Reactive

Some people will initiate a conversation others will wait until the time is right.

Example

....
....
....

Environment: Independent/Proximity/Cooperative

Some people like to work independently and have sole responsibility and their productivity suffers if they are asked to work with others, others seek a clear territory of responsibility but need to have others involved or around them or in proximity, their productivity will suffer too if they have to share responsibility or work alone and others want to share responsibility with others and may have problems in keeping to deadlines if they have to work alone, as managers they will want to do everything with their employees.

Example

....
....
....

Rule Structure: My/My

My/.:

No/My

My/Your

Some people have rules for both themselves and others. Others have rules for themselves and don't really care about others. Others have no rules for themselves but when given rules will pass them on to others and need others to set the rules and there is a fourth type that have rules for themselves but would feel uncomfortable sharing them with others or communicating them to others and are characterised by being able to appreciate both sides of an argument.

Example

....
....
....

Convincer:

Channel: See/Hear/Read/Do

Some people need to see a product, service or idea to be convinced while others need to hear it in an oral presentation. Then there are others who need to read on a product, service or idea to be convinced and there is a fourth type that needs to do something, possibly test a product or service to be convinced.

Example

....
....
....

Mode: No of Times or Examples/ Automatic/Consistent/Period of Time

Some people seek data a certain number of times to be convinced or learn something while others take a small amount of information and decide immediately based on what they imagine the rest to be and may jump to conclusions. Others are never completely convinced and need to re-evaluate every time, and there is a fourth type that need to gather information for a certain duration before being convinced.

Example

....
....
....

Content Sorts: People/Things/Information/Location

Some people organise their experience around people, others around things, others around information and others around location.

Example

....
....
....

REVIEW OF THE 'STACKING ANCHORS TECHNIQUE'

To stack anchors it is necessary to elicit several instances of states and anchor them in the same place.

The states chosen for a particular stacked anchor can be the same or different.

Future Pace "Can you imagine a time in the future when you might be in a similar situation, and what happens?"

THE GUIDED SEARCH TECHNIQUE - RECOVERING POWERFUL RESOURCE STATES/ EXPERIENCES FROM THE PAST

We can identify a positive state which we would like to have more of in our future and anchor it and then use that anchor to take us back in time finding the many other instances we can find of that state and stack anchors and then projecting ourselves into the future future pace those resources.

THE CHANGE PERSONAL HISTORY TECHNIQUE

The purpose of this technique is to utilise anchoring to help resolve a problem state/feeling or other unresourceful behaviour that is recurring in various contexts.

Identify a situation or context where you are less resourceful than you'd like to be or where there is a recurring unpleasant feeling that you would like to resolve, access the state and anchor it. Then hold the anchor down and go back in time to remember other times where you had the same kind of feelings and dissociating from the experience watch it as an adult, seeing the younger self, with all their adult resources available.

SEQUENCING

In NLP, the order and sequence in which we use our representational systems will get us different outcomes.

Regarding Sequencing Order, our sensory system is sequenced in various orders to achieve specific tasks efficiently. Driving a vehicle requires the visual sense to lead physical action for steering braking etc. V => K. The other senses, auditory (A) smell (O) taste (G) are less or not needed.

Driving a vehicle by physically acting first and looking last K => V results in accidents.

Sensory sequencing applies to every task we do.

It has been considered that emotional depression may be the result of thinking in a particular order and that depression, phobias and obsessions are the result of the order in which repetitive particular thoughts associated with conscious or unconscious images and feelings give rise to unwanted experiences.

RE-SEQUENCING

In NLP, Re-sequencing is the process of seeking out the specific sequencing order of thoughts and images that give rise to psychological problems and modifying the order in such a way that problems no longer occur.

Let's quickly look at the following example:

If someone is driving a vehicle, by acting first and looking last, accidents are caused; by changing the order around, looking first then acting we avoid the accidents. This simple process can be done without the need to reveal or repeat the content related to the unwanted outcome or experience.

Many who practice traditional counselling try to change or modify the content of a Client's problem without checking if the core of a Client's problem is the internal sensory order or sequence in which the content is processed rather than the content itself.

Changing the content of a Client's problem is similar to trying to change the past which is impossible, whereas changing the sequencing order in which the content is conveyed is dealing with the problem in the present.

It has been argued that traditional psychology could be criticised for not having paid enough attention to the order of sensory sequencing in which content is conveyed.

RIGHT CORE QUESTIONS AND CORE QUESTIONING

To make sure that your Core Questions serve you well there are several things to consider:

1. Think about what is presupposed or assumed.
2. Don't use Modal Operators of Necessity or Impossibility (should, must, ought, want, will, need, can, etc.) as they are usually limiting.
3. It is usually best to use Present and Future Verb Tenses.
4. Use of Self/Other Emphasis Pronouns (I, You, They, We).
5. Avoid Negations.
6. Avoid Comparisons (better, best, enough, more, less, etc.).
7. Make sure it cannot be answered with yes/no. If so it may be very limiting.
8. Does it direct the person towards a specific behaviour? If so make sure it directs them to the Present or Future.

PROGRAMMING YOUR FUTURE WITH A GOAL THAT YOU'D LIKE TO ACHIEVE WHILE REMOVING PRE-PROGRAMMED PROBLEMS IN THE FUTURE

We can float above our timeline and into the future and identify some future events that we are sure will be there and notice what we have inadvertently programmed into our future that shouldn't be there (an illness, a problem, a negative state or experience) and change any negative states or experiences by modifying them to become a resource/resourceful state or experience, eliminating them or replacing the unwanted event with one that is preferred and fully associating into it to getting the feelings and then dropping it into the right place on the timeline to establish it there and then floating again above the timeline and see ourself in the event in a revised way.

Another exercise we could do is to identify a goal and to contrast it with the present state, apply well formed conditions and then make sure that the goal is ecological by asking: What will happen if I get my goal? What will happen if I don't get it? What won't happen if I get it? What won't happen if I don't get it?

We could represent the goal in all three systems (auditorily, visually and kinaesthetically)

We could float out above the timeline to the place where we want to have achieve the goal and float down on the timeline at the appropriate future moment and fully experience it, making sure that the submodalities are just right and when it seems ideal to step back out of the experience to see ourself in the event, and notice how all the events between then and the present are changing and rearranging themselves as to fully support the change wanted. Then return to the present, associate into it and look at the event in the future realising and noticing that this is just the beginning of what we want and seeing that this event establishes a direction into the future for having more and more of this kind of thing in life.

We could identify any resources that might be needed to accomplish the goal and float back to a time when we had the resource and relive it fully and then float forward on the timeline beyond the present and to the appropriate place on their timeline and place it there so that resource is supporting achieving the goal.

RECODING EXPERIENCES

When we transform our experiences into our internal representations or internal maps, we code and store them in our mind in certain particular patterns.

We can code our experiences in any number of ways; if the way we've coded a particular experience proves to be less useful than we would like, we can recode it in a more useful way.

As we say in NLP, "We are the cartographers of our own map of reailty", and, we can change the map in any way we choose to, so, what better than to change it so that it more usefully serves our purposes.

In NLP we use submodality techniques to recode our experiences in such a way that we can make those useful changes easily, quickly and gracefully; Submodalities are key components to many of the NLP change techniques.

Submodalities by themselves or together with other techniques are used to assist Clients to quit smoking, eat more of certain foods and less of others, address compulsion issues, change beliefs and values, enhance motivation, move from stress to relaxation, address phobias, etc.

Recoding those submodalities is recoding decisions.

RECODING SUBMODALITIES IS RECODING DECISIONS

recoding of decisions can be easily done using positive imprints that we create or by taking our present self back in time to just before a bad experience took place

In NLP we say "If I knew then what I know now."

We can think of a positive imprint/experience and identify it's submodalities and then search for a negative imprint experience and the decision that resulted from it that affects life at present in a way we don't like.

Then we think of a generalisation or attitude that gets in the way and do a guided search back through time to find the imprint experience that formed it.

Then think about what imprint experience, if it had come earlier, would have coloured the past in a very positive way, so that when we went through the unuseful imprint experience we would have automatically interpreted it in a different way and responded more resourcefully.

CHAPTER 2
MODELLING

STATE CHAINING

State Chaining is all about Chaining State Anchors.

Let's review 'Chaining Anchors' and when we would you use the technique.

In NLP, Chaining Anchors is a sequencing of a series of states; if we have set up a few anchors, we can fire them off one after the other changing the state as each emotion is at it's peak and moving through a sequence of states.

An anchor chaining will make a Client go through different states automatically with the first state inducing a process that automatically leads to the last state and it is used when the desired/resource state is significantly different from the present state which is a stuck state.

GAINING EXPERIENCE WITH FULL BODY PACING

If we can identify something that we don't do well, we can think of the state (horse-riding and sight-seeing) and we put ourself in that state by using a kinaesthetic, noticing the submodalities experienced in this state. We can learn to do so many things just by using a kinaesthetic lead (walking pace, posture, breathing, movement of the arms).

"Glitches in perceptual and thinking processes cause impoverished and inadequate
mental maps of reality."
Noam Chomsky

"Taking multiple perspectives, literally, on any one issue gives you the foundation for wisdom."

"A single perspective of any problem is automatically wrong."
"A single perspective cannot hope to capture all the subtleties and
complexities that are characteristic of real problems."
William James

CRITICAL PATTERNS OF CHANGE

Looking at an event from different points of reference has its benefits and these are:

1. There is no right perspective in any situation
2. Not everyone shares our point of view
3. You build understanding from different perspectives

In NLP there are three valuable tools to use when faced with a personal or business related problem where a Client feels stuck or unresourceful:

1. Neurological Levels (Environment, Behaviours, Capabilities, Beliefs/Values, Identity, Spiritual)
2. Timeframes (Past, Present, Future)
3. Perceptual Positions (Self, Other, Observer)

Let's explore how the problem changes as we shift Neurological Levels, Timeframes and Perceptual Positions.

THE SIX NEUROLOGICAL LEVELS OF CHANGE

The six logical levels of change as seen before are:

1. Environment
2. Behaviour
3. Capabilities and Skills
4. Beliefs and Values
5. Identity
6. Purpose/Spiritual

A change that happens at a higher level usually reflects back at some of the lower levels.

When looking for the cause why a change is not happening, it is usually useful to look at the neurological levels and see where exactly the block to the change is located.

Environment

If a person wants to lose weight, he may have to find a good gym to workout. If the gym is not available in his neighbourhood, then he faces the difficulty at the environment level.

Behaviour

This is what a person does. What would a person DO, in order to lose weight? He would practice going for a walk everyday.

Capabilities and Skills

Does the person have the necessary capabilities and skills to make the change?

Beliefs and Values

Is the person's Belief System in alignment with his outcome?

Identity

Is what the person thinks of himself/herself in alignment with his outcome? This region is about the various roles we play in our lives.

Purpose

Is the purpose for losing the weight which is the ultimate outcome.

Exercise – Neurological Levels

Problem: Tommy's behaviour has been an issue at school.

Let's try solving the problem using Neurological Levels:

Let's say you have identified the problem as being Behavioural

Environment   Behaviours Capabilities Beliefs/Values Identity Purpose/Spiritual/Transcendental

Look at it from Environment, Capabilities, Beliefs/Values, Identity, and Purpose/Spiritual/ Transcendental.

Tommy as we know is having behavioural issues at school, this is how the situation is manifesting itself.(Behaviours)

Tommy might be behaving badly because the class environment is poor. (environment)

Tommy might be behaving badly because he feels left out of class activities. (capability)

Tommy might be behaving badly due to his upbringing. (beliefs/values)

Tommy might be behaving badly because he feels he doesn't fit in. (identity)

Tommy might be behaving badly because he feels disconnected and alone and lacks a sense of oneness, of purpose. (Purpose/Spiritual/Transcendental)

TIMEFRAMES ON THE TIMELINE

Our timeline contains all timeframes, it contains the present, the here and now, it contains what has happened in the past and it contains what is to happen in the future.

When eliciting a Client's timeline we elicit all timeframes and then it's just a matter of positioning them in the present past and future to gather different perspectives/information; Emotions are known to change when we adopt a different position on the timeline.

Exercise: Timeframes

Problem: Michael seems distracted now/in the present.

Let's try solving the problem using Timeframes

←==================================O================================→

Past   **Present**   **Future**

Michael could be distracted because he can't help remembering how he failed his math test last semester. (Past)

Michael could be distracted because he is anxious about his next math test. (Future)

Exercise

Problem: Sonia is finding it hard to concentrate on her work this semester.

Let's get more information on what could be wrong using Timeframes:

←==================================O============================→

Past   **Present**   **Future**

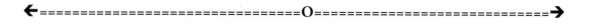

Depression **Anxiety**

Sonia might be depressed about something that happened in her past.

Sonia might be anxious about her upcoming holiday break.

Always state the 'Problem' in the Present to begin with when working with Timeframes.

THE THREE PERCEPTUAL POSITIONS – THE TRIPLE DESCRIPTION

NLP's Perceptual Positions is an NLP process for discovering different points of view on any situation and works really well in situations where one has an awkward conversation with someone, or when one is not getting on with someone.

The First Perceptual Position is all about a Client looking at the world from their own point of view and through their own eyes fully associated and without taking account of anyone else's point of view. The question we would ask them while in this position is 'How does this affect you?'

The Second Perceptual Position is all about how it would look, feel, sound for someone else, looking through another person's eyes and considering their point of view. The question you would ask a Client while in this position is: 'How would this appear to them?'

Rapport with another person will make it easier to appreciate their reality and achieve the Second Perceptual Position.

The Third Position is all about observing from a completely uninvolved and dissociated position. The question you would ask a Client while in this position is 'How would this look to someone who is not involved?'

From going through the three perceptual positions, the information gathered creates an objective viewpoint from which we would be able to generate and evaluate some useful choices in a difficult situation.

All three "perceptual positions" are important and the purpose of using all three is to gain what we call in NLP a 'Triple Description'.

Exercise

Problem: I (self) disagree with Jack's point of view and Tania watches us argue.

Let's try solving the problem using Perceptual Positions:

O==============================➜=============================➜

  Me (Self)   Jack (Other)   Tania (Observer)

I decide to consider Jacks point of view (Other) and or Tania's point of view (Observer)

I decide to put myself in Jacks place or in Tania's place or both and see how I feel being them.

Jack's position is still an associated position, Tania's position is a totally dissociated and unattached perspective.

SLEIGHT OF MOUTH PATTERNS (POWERFUL SET OF REFRAMING PATTERNS)

In NLP, Sleight of Mouth Patterns are reframing patterns identified by Robert Dilts from some of Richard Bandlers Language Patterns and they are a system of 14 different patterns of response to a stated belief.

Their use loosens the boundaries that Client's may have built up and they are used as an advanced language technique to overcome objections.

These patterns assist Clients in expanding their model of the world so that other possibilities can be considered.

The value of any Sleight of Mouth response should be viewed in terms of whether or not it helps the Client and something to keep in mind is that for a particular intervention you wouldn't use them all, you would use a sub-set that best supports your Client.

While studying the patterns you will find that you have used each of them at one time or another, however you will benefit from being able to generate a response using any of the 14 patterns or reframes as this will give you flexibility in responding to a Client.

Sleight of Mouth patterns work well for belief change, hence, in order to use Sleight of Mouth patterns the Client's belief must first be expressed as a complex equivalence or cause-effect assertion so make sure you do that first.

ELICITING THE CLIENT'S BELIEF WITH QUESTIONS

To elicit a Client's full belief you might want to assist them by asking them questions such as:

"What does .... mean to you?"

"What are the consequences of ....?"

"What will ....lead to?"

If your Client responds with a complex equivalence or cause effect, then you have something to work with and can proceed to apply a Sleight of Mouth pattern.

Let's quickly look at all 14 patterns:

1. Intention – What could be the positive intention??? Direct attention to the purpose or intention of the belief.

2. Redefine – Use words that are similar but may infer something different. Substitute a new word for one of the words used in the belief statement that means something similar but has different implications.

3. Consequence/s – Focus on a consequence that leads to challenging the belief. Direct attention to an effect of the belief or the relationship defined by the belief.

4. Chunk down – Look at a specific element that challenges the belief. Break down the elements of the belief into small enough pieces that it changes the relationship defined by the belief.

5. Chunk up – Generalise in order to change the relationship defined by the belief. Generalise an element of the belief to a larger classification that changes the relationship defined by the belief.

6. Counter example – Find an exception that challenges the generalisation defined by the belief. Find an example that does not fit the relationship defined by the belief.

7. Metaphor or Analogy – Use an analogy or metaphor that challenges the generalisation defined by the belief. Find a relationship analogous to that defined by the belief, but which has different implications.

8. Apply to self – Use key aspects of the belief to challenge the belief. Evaluate the belief statement it'self according to the relationship or criteria defined by the belief.

9. Another outcome – Propose a different outcome that challenges the relevancy of the belief. Challenge the relevancy of the belief and switch to another issue altogether.

10. Hierarchy of criteria – Re-assess the belief based on a more important criterion. Reevaluate the belief according to a criterion that is more important than any addressed by the belief.

11. Change frame size – Re-evaluate the implication of the belief in the context of a longer or shorter time frame, a larger number of people or from an individual point of view or a bigger or smaller perspective.

12. Meta-frame – Challenge the basis for the belief/formulate a belief as to the origin of the belief. Evaluate the belief from the frame of an ongoing, personally oriented context establishing a belief about the belief.

13. Model of the world – Look at the belief from a different perspective or model of the world/from someone else's perspective and reevaluate the belief from the framework of a different model of the world.

14. Reality strategy – Re-assess the belief based on the fact that beliefs are based on specific perceptions/ask 'what specifically' and reevaluate the belief accounting for the fact that people operate from cognitive perceptions of the world to build beliefs.

These Sleight of Mouth Patterns or reframing can also be applied to self-talk and they can make someone more resourceful in addressing any issues they may be facing and will certainly assist in expanding their view of the world.

Reframing is also an excellent way to handle questions and objections, not just belief change.

Reframing changes the meaning a Client has associated with a particular piece of information, it allows for them to change their subjective meaning.

Sleight of Mouth patterns or reframes are best used in combination rather than individually, however, we wouldn't use every pattern in one intervention, only the subset that best suit's the Client.

Sleight of Mouth patterns are a valuable tool for persuasion also because they can help Clients overcome limiting beliefs, open up to new ideas and find a new spin or point of view to a situation.

Almost any interaction with people can be improved and we can also use these patterns to overcome our own self-limiting beliefs too.

The power of Sleight of Mouth is that it gives us more choices and flexibility of possible responses, and with 14 different responses you will never be at a loss for something to say.

While this is a set of powerful tools for someone like a sales person or a lawyer, they are also useful for a hypnotherapist or NLP Practitioner in many ways; a Client's beliefs about therapy or hypnosis could inhibit their cooperation in the therapeutic process, sometimes a negative belief about life or health is all that is stopping a Client from making some progress, and, creating enough expectation in the client's mind of what the hypnosis will mean the job is half done before the formal hypnosis even begins.

Exercise

In conversation someone tells you that their partner spends too much time on social media so you ask them the questions that will enable you to elicit from them a belief stated as a complex equivalence or cause effect.

QUESTIONS TO ASK

Formulate the questions you would ask below.

"What does .... mean to you?"

"What are the consequences of ....?"

"What will .... lead to?"

COMPLEX EQUIVALENCE OR CAUSE EFFECT RESPONSES FROM CLIENT

Formulate your Client's three possible responses below.

1..

2..

3..

PROCEED TO SLEIGHT OF MOUTH

Proceed to apply Sleight of Mouth pattern selecting the subset of patterns or reframes that would best suit your Client. You have more room on the next page to continue.

Remember that there will be as you know two parts to the responses from the questions (a part A and a part B. In Sleight of Mouth patterns we can focus on either A or B or both.)

PROBLEM IDENTIFICATION AND SOLVING STRATEGY

If we identify an experience where we have reached a deadlock and select a physical location to be associated with it we can then associate into that experience as fully as possible and step into the physical location we have chosen.

Then we can step away from the physical location and visualise the system involved in the deadlock experience (including environment, mechanical elements of the system and the information carrying system) and visualise the information influencing the system as colours flowing through the system and to find where exactly it is that the flow gets blocked or stuck identifying if there is a diffusion, damping, deviation, loss of impetus, break of continuity or impossibility of transformation; and find a reference in the experience for a functional system selecting a different physical location for it and associating into the positive reference experience stepping into the location chosen for it.

Then step away from the positive reference location and visualise the differences in the information flow of that system and then using the functional references experience as guide to visualise a way to refocus the information, remove resistance, redirect, strengthen source, reconnect or find a new pathway.

THE USE OF PICTURES FOR LANDSCAPING A PROBLEM AND FINDING A SOLUTION

If we can identify a problem or goal we can draw a picture representing our understanding of the landscape of the problem or goal. (The picture may be a sketch or a symbolic representation.)

Then identify an area of potential solution and make a statement using the meta model inquiries, sleight of mouth, presuppositions, NLP Presuppositions or verb tense shifts and make a representation of the solution that would be most valuable by either drawing a new picture, adding to the previous one and think of a metaphor or analogy to the representation.

GEO - A STRATEGY FOR EFFECTIVENESS

Use of the following questions can be very useful in achieving goals:

- What do you do in order to reach your goals?
- What do you do if you are not satisfactorily reaching your goals?
- How do you know when you have achieved your goals?
- How do you know it is time to stop and move on to something else

HOW TO USE GEO

We can apply GEO to identify problem areas and make adjustments that will result in effectiveness within a problem context.

We think of two contexts, one where we do well and are effective and the other a similar context where we are less effective and we contrast the two using the following questions:

a. What do we do in order to reach our goals?
b. What do we do if we are not satisfactorily reaching our goals?
c. How do we know when we have achieved our goals?
d. How do we know it is time to stop and move on to something else

Then we make the goal in the ineffective context the same as the goal in the effective context and notice how this changes the evidence and methods for achieving the goal in the once ineffective context. We can revise if necessary the methods and evidence to be more like the ones in their effective context.

SYNAESTHESIAS

Synaesthesia means 'a synthesising of the senses, and, it is an automatic link from one sense to another.

When a Client seems to use two representational systems at the same time, indicating visual eye movements but using kinaesthetic predicates and body language, this is a 'Synaesthesia'.

Synaesthesia is actually two or more representational systems at work together.

When a sound has a feel or texture or colour we have a synaesthesia.

A strong memory may produce a negative kinaesthetic feeling linked with a positive visual memory and the Client doesn't understand why they feel the way they do; this is another synaesthesia.

Clients with synaesthesia usually have good memories, and the more sensory 'recordings' we can call upon, the better we recall memories.

Clients with extraordinary memories tend to use more than one representational system synesthetically and memories mirror real, multisensory life in the same way a vivid imagination operates in multisensory mode.

Synaesthesias are a significant part of how people organise reality. We perceive the world that we live in through our five senses, sight, sound, feeling, taste and smell; NLP combines Olfatory and Gustatory together within the Kinaesthetic category leaving three categories which in NLP is abbreviated as VAK.

People tend to have a primary or 'lead' representational system they begin with and they stay in one modality more than the other two.

Behaviour and language matches the system the individual is operating from at any particular time. An individual operating in Visual will use visual predicates in their language.

When an activity in one representational system initiates activity in another representational system we have a synaesthesia. For example a harsh sound (auditory) can cause an individual to feel uncomfortable (kinaesthetic).

Synaesthesias constitute how we make meaning from the world around us. Synaesthesia is thought to be at the root of many complex processes including knowledge, choice, and communication.

Many of the biggest differences between people's talents, abilities, and skills are a consequence of the order and sequence of these representational system correlations.

In private consultation, an NLP Practitioner might help a Client unpack a problem state held in place by a synaesthesia, by helping them take it apart and then re-representing the Visual, Auditory, and Kinaesthetic parts of the problem state the client can get some freedom of choice to notice that the individual parts do not have the same power; with the synaesthesias unpacked, a client can then reframe the problem state to a more resourceful state with new behaviours.

SYNAESTHESIA AND OVERLAPPING

In NLP, "overlap" has to do with the connections between the senses. For example we can "overlap" an image and a sound together. Sounds or images may also be overlapped onto feelings.

It is important to notice that Overlap is possible because our sensory experiences become mixed together in our nervous systems and it is this connecting together of information from the different senses that makes creativity and learning possible.

The process of overlap, makes it possible to form cognitive strategies in which sensory processes and representations are linked together in a particular sequence.

Experiences which involve an overlap of the senses are usually richer and more powerful than perceiving something through a single sense alone. Many of the most powerful experiences in our lives such as 'religious' or 'spiritual' experiences we know now involve an integrating together of the various senses.

Overlap is used in many NLP processes to create or enrich a particular experience.

To create a resource state, for example, a Client may be instructed to "Visualise how they would look if they were able to act effectively and resourcefully." When they are able to form an image, the picture may be overlapped onto the kinaesthetic representational system by suggesting, "As you watch yourself in that image, notice what feelings and body sensations accompany those actions." Then, the image and feelings would be overlapped onto the auditory system by asking, "If you had those feelings and sensations in your body, how would your voice sound? What sort of tone and rhythm goes with those feelings?"

SYNAESTHESIA AND CREATIVITY

Some versions of synaesthesia are sometimes called 'pseudo-synaesthesia', and for many Clients they are a part of their normal thinking processes. This kind of everyday synaesthesia is very common among artists and other creative types, like a lot of poets,

A grapheme-colour synaesthesia is one in which words (and numbers) are associated with particular colours.

Another type of synaesthesia is when an artist and/or writer, while writing a novel makes sketches of characters in the margin, the sketches are not just decorative, but an integral part of the process of generating dialogue.

Have you ever doodled on a piece of paper while talking on the phone?

Understanding synaesthesias can also help to communicate more effectively.

PARALLEL PROCESSING & DISCOVERING LEAD REPRESENTATIONAL SYSTEM

We can discover the lead representational system (V, A, K) after parallel processing engaging all three.

First we construct a chart with the alphabet from A to Z (5 columns by x 5 rows).

Then using the letters l, r and t, we put these under the letters of the alphabet (l under R, r under L, and t under anything but T. We then Sing the chart in different directions (forward, backward, in diagonal/cross lateral, +, x.) with an external tempo marker such as a hand clap, right hand left foot, left hand right foot (making use of V, A, and K). Mix it up. (There's no right way to do this and faster is not necessarily better.)

Then we Sing it deleting 2 letters without missing the beat. (When a miss is made we must return to the beginning of the alphabet and continue.) After doing this for 10 minutes, and, standing in the same physiological position we must think through our preference of lead representational system or VAK.

Which one are you? (See previous notes on Synaesthesias.)

CHAINING SYNAESTHESIAS TO CREATE NEW STRATEGY POSSIBILITIES/MENTAL PATTERNS OF CHOICE

We can chain synaesthesias to create new strategy possibilities to generate change.

If we can identify a problem context where we would like more choices and we fully associate with it we can then identify and access a resource state (a time when we were flexible and effective, that would make a difference in our behaviour) and we can then re-access the problem context and think about the content of the situation and holding it in mind exaggerate the physiology of the problem context and then shift physiology to that of the resource state, the problem context now has the resource state physiology and general aspects the problem context is no longer a problem, we now call it resourceful context/situation and we keep building on it synaesthesias such as move eyes to all quadrants rapidly in a figure eight while breathing fully and thinking about the resourceful context/ situation and/or move eyes to Vc/Ad while thinking through the resourceful context/ situation.

"Self-Change is Change we can believe in."

Ana Marcela Duarte

"Before you exceed anyone's expectations

You need to first exceed your own expectations of yourself."

Ana Marcela Duarte

"Do not measure your life by your goals, but by
what you are doing to achieve them."

Peter Drucker

MODELLING

Modelling is the science of achieving excellence by copying the exact process (including the thought process) of a person. According to Richard Bandler there are three components to excellence:

1. The Belief System of a person or the Six Logical Levels of Change.
2. The Syntax of a thought process.
3. The physiology of the person.

These are what we model.

Modelling is the core of NLP and NLP has developed basically through Modelling.

Richard Bandler and John Grinder formulated NLP by Modelling successful therapists like Milton Erickson and Virgina Sattire.

MODELLING EFFECTIVE BEHAVIOUR FROM EFFECTIVE PERFORMERS

We can all Model effective behaviour from effective performers.

We can identify the GEOs of an effective performer by asking them a set of questions:.

a. What are your goals?
b. How do you know you are achieving your goals?
c. What do you do in order to reach your goals?
d. What do you do if you are not satisfactorily reaching your goals?

Then we can identify the effective performer's physiology and identify criteria, values, and internal representations that the effective performer uses while performing, and then with all the information gathered we can fully imagine a context where we would like to have the new effective behaviour fully available and see ourselves in the context behaving with the new behaviour.

We need to check for congruity and to modify the behaviour if an incongruity is found.

We can work on the context until it feels write and fully associate into the context.

We can then Test/Futurepace by imagining a time in the future when we might be in a similar situation, and what happens.

The following exercise is another example of Modelling practice.

Exercise:

1. Identify an example of the behaviour to be Modelled.
2. Identify it's GEO.
3. Identify it's Perceptual Positioning.
4. Identify consideration of time/sense of time.
5. Identify Neurological Level (especially beliefs and identity required).
6. Identify necessary Physiology (posture, gestures, eye accessing cues, autonomic cues.
7. Identify submodalities.
8. Identify Meta-Model Distinctions.
9. Identify Meta-programs
10. Identify relationships with others.
11. Identify General State Description.
12. **Futurepace the new behaviour (state and strategy) by rehearsing it in the appropriate future contexts, first from a meta-position and dissociated and then fully associated.**

FROM DOUBT TO RESONANCE BUILDING

We can make an experience in a problem context of doubt shift to resonating with our positive mentors or in response to their influence by identifying a situation in which we experience doubt or self-doubt about our beliefs or mission and to relive the negative experience and then adopting a meta-position (other or observer) acknowledge 3 mentors that had an impact in our life influencing us in a positive way by resonating, releasing or unveiling something deep inside us (relating to identity, commitment and love respectively). We surround the mentors around ourself in the context in which we experience doubt and then physically associate into each of the mentors one at a time and to send a message (as if each mentor) to ourself (the self in doubt).

We go to the observer position and identify the meta-message behind the messages of each of the mentors, we find the common message that resonates within the messages from all three mentors and then once again associate into each mentor and to communicate as if them the common message to the self in doubt.

CHAPTER 3

BELIEFS AND CHANGE

WHAT ARE LIMITING BELIEFS?

We have learnt that Limiting Beliefs are beliefs that constrain us in some way, that limit us from thinking saying or doing the things that they inhibit and therefore lead us to living an impoverished life. We know that Limiting Beliefs can be beliefs about rights, duties, abilities, permissions etc...

We know Limiting Beliefs are often about ourself and our self-identity and that they can also be about other people and the world around us. We can and do many times define ourselves and the world around us in a very limiting way. Lets look at why we limit our beliefs.

WHY DO WE LIMIT OUR BELIEFS?

It is partly through our direct experiences that we limit our beliefs, and, for the most part, they can be very helpful; they can also be very limiting if we form false and limiting conclusions.

Education tells us what is right and wrong, good and bad from a very early age, helping us survive and grow, but it also may limit us from useful experiences and knowledge.

Limiting beliefs are very often driven by fear with a very strong social component to our decisions and the thought of criticism, ridicule and rejection by others which is enough to powerfully inhibit us.

We may also fear harm in some way by others and either avoid them or seek to appease them.

In order to overcome limiting beliefs we need to identify them and act to change what we believe.

How we believe drives our actions; what and how we believe has a huge impact on what we do and whether we succeed and so special attention on beliefs and limiting beliefs is a must.

LIMITING BELIEFS AND ENABLING BELIEFS

Limiting Beliefs can hold us back in life but we can also have enabling beliefs that help us forward. Enabling beliefs lead us to growth, success and happiness.

There are several types of enabling belief.

Probability Beliefs: Example: "This might work. So it's worth giving it a go".

Ability Beliefs: Example: "I can get there. I just need to keep going."

Existence Beliefs: Example: "I'm intelligent. If I work hard, I can learn most things."

Respect Beliefs: Example: "I am a person who accepts others as they are. This will lead to me having many good friends."

THE CHOICE IS OURS

We have the choice of either reviewing our limiting beliefs and eliminating them or converting them to enabling beliefs. We can also look for other enabling beliefs to adopt.

You can help your Clients by looking for the beliefs that hold them back and encouraging them to adopt enabling beliefs.

SOME OF THE MAJOR NLP PRESUPPOSITIONS ARE ENABLING BELIEFS

One of my trainers asks me "How much progress have you made?". He is presupposing that I have made progress. Presuppositions are a powerful form of subliminal communication.

As seen before, NLP has certain presuppositions and it can be said that these presuppositions are the pillars of NLP. Let's review them:

- Each person has a unique perception of the world.
- Each person makes the best choice available to them at the time they make it.
- People work perfectly.
- Everything is feedback.
- Every behaviour of yours (and others) has a positive intention.
- The meaning of the communication is it's effect (the result you get).
- There is a solution to every problem.
- We have all the resources within us.
- The Map is not the territory.
- He who has the greatest flexibility has the greatest influence.
- Mind and Body are one.
- Excellence can be duplicated.
- What we see in others, is true about ourselves.
- Knowledge, thought, memory and imagination are the result of sequences and combinations of ways of filtering and storing information.
- Experience is the best teacher, we learn NLP not by theoretical study, but by experiencing it.

BELIEFS OF EXCELLENCE THAT WE CAN MODEL

There are some basic beliefs of excellence that we can model. Some useful beliefs to hold are:

- Whatever happens has a purpose, and there is a reason behind every happening.
- There is no such thing as failure.
- Whatever happens, take responsibility.
- It is not necessary to understand everything in order to be able to use everything.
- People are the greatest resource.
- Work is play.
- There is no abiding success without commitment.

USEFUL BELIEFS

There is an easy way to either identify or create useful beliefs and that is by following these Rules:

1. Useful beliefs are stated in simple language or childlike language.
2. Useful beliefs are stated in the positive.
3. Useful beliefs are NOT the opposite of the limiting belief.
4. Useful beliefs add behavioural choices.
5. Useful beliefs are ecological, meaning you cannot predict a downside to living with the new belief.

Exercise: Review 2 current beliefs below

State Current Belief 1 ....

Analyse Current Belief 1 ....

....

....

....

....

....

State Current Belief 2 ....

Analyse Current Belief 2 ....
....
....
....
....
....
....

Exercise: Create 2 New Beliefs

State New Belief 1 ....

Analyse the New Belief ....
....
....
....
....
....

State New Belief 2 ....

Analyse the New Belief ....
....
....
....
....
....

IDENTIFYING LIMITING BELIEFS AND CHANGING INTERNAL REPRESENTATIONS

The way to change our internal representations is a simple process: We identify a Present/Problematic State and we ask ourselves "How is that a problem?", and we identify the Meta Model Violations/language patterns (deletions, distortions, generalisations) in our answer/description of the Present/Problematic State (Some of the most commonly problematic Meta Model violations are: Mind Reading, Modal Operators, Cause and Effect, and Complex Equivalence.).

Then we develop the Meta Model Responses/Questions. Just as our mental maps operate by deleting, distorting and generalising information, the Meta Model provides a series of questions designed to unravel the Distortions, Generalisations and Deletions that took place in the communication.

(What specifically? Whom specifically? Who?, How?, Where? & When?)

The process will change our internal representations.

RE-IMPRINTING

In NLP. we know that an imprint is a significant experience or period of life from the past in which a person formed a belief or cluster of beliefs, often determining their identity. It often involves the unconscious role-Modelling of significant others (family members and teachers).

The purpose of reimprinting is not only to resolve the emotional issues associated with a particular event but to find the resources to change the beliefs that were formed during the imprinting.

There is a process in NLP whereby we identify the most important resource or belief we would have needed as our younger self, we anchor that resource and we take it back to the location on the timeline before an imprint occurred. We take the resource into our younger self and walk all the way up the timeline to the present, verbalizing its effect throughout our life and experiencing the changes made by the reimprinting. Can we take this a step further? Yes we can by walking all the way into the future and seeing the effects of the new reimprint in the future. And it is important to note here that we don't need to change anyone else's imprint just our own which we do with the reimprinting. Reimprinting will occur before the imprint took place. What we do is give our younger self the resources we would have needed then but didn't have to empower us to respond differently to any situations throughout our timeline.

REIMPRINTING A PAST EXPERIENCE

Often when we can identify a limiting belief we can also identify a negative imprint somewhere in our past. There is an exercise we can do to replace old imprints with new experiences caused by the reimprinting:

Exercise:

First identify a negative state and how you feel while standing in the present and facing the future.

We focus on the state and the beliefs associated with it.

Then we start to slowly walk backwards pausing at any location that seems to be relevant to that state and the beliefs that accompany it.

We continue to walk backwards until we reach the earliest experience associated with the state and belief and we Verbalise how we feel *"I am feeling …..."*

We consider what resources were missing in ourself our younger self.

We then Observe the imprint experience from meta-position/observer noticing the effect that the earlier experience has had on our life and we Verbalise about the events we experienced in third person, past tense *"The younger me thought..."*, "The younger me needed……."

Then we identify the most important resource or belief we would have needed as our younger self and we anchor it and take it back to the location on the timeline before the imprint occurred. We take the resource into our younger self verbalizing what we would have said and done instead, and then from our younger self we walk all the way up our timeline to the present, experiencing the changes made by the reimprinting. We can also walk all the way into the future and experience the changes that the reimprinting will have on our future, what do you hear see and feel in those future situations?. This is the way to future pace the effects of the reimprinting.

REIMPRINGING - UPDATING ROLE-MODELS

Sometimes as part of the reimprinting we will see the upgrading of role-models, I do this separately to avoid confusion.

Exercise:

First idendify a limiting belief you have had for a long time, this is a belief which is not empowering and enabling, it often has a negative imprint at the root, an experience of something said by someone with that belief that affected you in a negative way.

Follow that limiting belief backwards through all the instances in which it might have affected you right to the very first you can remember as your younger self.

When you have identified the first instance step off your timeline and in 3rd position as observer observe how that limiting belief has affected your life.

Think of an empowering role model and anchor their words while on the timeline in the present and take them back to your younger self just before the imprint of the negative experience occurred and imagine the new role model speaking to you with enabling empowering words, notice what you see hear and feel and anchor that.

Travel along your timeline with your new role model through every negative experience with those words of encouragement that empower you. Go right through your timeline until the present and keep going into the future, future pacing the empowering words in situations where you might need them, focus on what you see hear and feel in those situations.

Go back to the present and step off the timeline and observe what a difference those words have made to your life.

ADDRESSING 'PARTS' - INTEGRATING CONFLICTING BELIEF SYSTEMS

In NLP, we know that Emotional Experiences throughout life, and especially during the early imprint years can result in the creation of Parts at an unconscious level; they generate their own values and beliefs, and are responsible for certain behaviours.

Many overwhelming feelings, reactions and out of control behaviours are caused by Conflicting Parts.

When two or more Parts of a person lead to behaviours which are contradictory, Internal Conflicts occur, and, problematic conflicts occur when the opposing parts have negative judgments about each other.

The resolution to the conflict comes from identifying a common positive intention.

NLP's popular Parts Integration technique is one of the most useful skills to overcome bad habit's, indecision, procrastination and all sorts of internal conflicts creating harmony between Parts of the unconscious mind so that their values are in alignment - a person with 'Integrated Parts' is more congruent, empowered and clear in their decisions and actions.

Exercise:

We start off by establishing the unwanted behaviour or indecision and then we identify at least two opposing Parts, the Part that wants to change and the Part that keeps doing the problem.

Then we create an image of both Parts and we place them one in each hand.

We ask the Parts for their intentions until they arrive at a positive value and then we notice that what both Parts want (their highest intention) is either identical or compatible.

Then we elicit each Parts' resources and we have the hands turn towards each other and see the two internal images begin to merge as the hands progressively move closer together to create a third image that symbolises the integration of the two former Parts.

We then bring the new integrated image into our body through placing both hands on our heart, breathing it in and absorbing this whole new experience and being a more integrated person.

And finally we can consider how we're going to approach any problematic situation differently in the future, now that the Parts are fully integrated…

This process can be repeated until all Parts are 'playing for the same team'.

Remember – we are more than the sum of our Parts.

FOREGROUND/BACKGROUND SWITCH

What are we focusing on when as we think of a current problem or issue?

If the issue involves another person, in our mind we may have a big bright close-up picture of him or her., and if we were to replay their voice in our mind we may hear it loud and clear with a specific tone that results in us feeling upset for instance. All of this is in our foreground.

However, there is also other information in the background like resources that we don't pay attention to which are very useful to have at hand. There is much we choose not to see hear or feel as clearly or at all.

What would happen if we put less focus or attention on what is in the foreground and more focus or attention on what is in the background? Maybe the problem or issue would not seem so big and overwhelming and as a result we would be more resourceful.

In NLP there is a foreground/background technique which is a simple process that assists us in becoming more aware of what is in the background so we can choose to give it more or all of our attention and therefore be more resourceful and aware of the multitude of choices we all have.

It consists of thinking first of a time when we experienced an issue. We focus on where we were and what we were seeing, hearing and doing and what precisely we noticed at that time being as specific as possible, all of this is in the foreground.

Then we think about what we might not have been aware of, what we did not notice, maybe all other objects in the room and we allow for all these things from the background to switch to the foreground and all that we are aware of to switch to the background.

The effect of this switch drives the client's attention from what they were paying attention to, to what they were not paying attention to.

As a result, the things they were paying attention to seem less important, and their problems seem less important.

Including an Outcome/WFO

We could also come up with a well formed outcome before beginning with the previous technique and we could state the WFO before doing the switch. By doing this we are priming the unconscious mind to set up a filter that will attract things that are supportive of the outcome.

When doing the switch the issue will seem much less serious than before the exercise, and using an outcome to directionalise our attention will create a positive state using the foreground-background switch.

COMPULSION BLOWOUT

In NLP there is also a technique to practice blowing out compulsions. It is all about doing a contrastive submodality analysis between two experiences, one in which we feel compelled to do something which we would rather not be compelled to do and the second an experience that is neutral, and, discovering as a result the most powerful analog submodality differences between the two. After doing this we decide which submodality can be used to increase the feeling of compulsion and we increase this submodality to it's maximum to blowout the compulsion. We can future pace the compulsion to future situations and if it is still present we can repeat this process of compulsion blowout.

CHANGING BELIEF SYSTEMS WITH NLP

As mentioned before, in his book 'Changing Belief Systems with NLP'. Robert Dilts' 'Neurological Level Alignment' identifies six different levels of experience corresponding to six different levels of neurological 'circuitry'.

1. Environment

Environment corresponds the 'where' our life takes place. Here we ask the question "Where does (whatever we're exploring) take place?"

2. Behaviour

The level of Behaviour has to do with our actions, what we say and do. Here we ask the question "what specifically do we do when we're engaged in (whatever we're exploring)?".

3. Capabilities

Capabilities is the area of our skills and knowledge and resources. The question to ask ourselves here is "How do we do (whatever we're exploring)?, and What capabilities and skills do we tap into when engaged in the area of our life we have chosen to explore?".

4. Beliefs and Values

The Beliefs and Values level is that of what we hold true, what we believe in and what we value, in other words what we stand for. Here we ask the question Why (whatever we're exploring)?, and this question will assist us in identifying our values and 'what's true about (whatever we're exploring)?'

5. Identity

The level of Identity is all about who we are The question we ask here is "Who are we when we are engaged in (whatever we're exploring)?".

6. Spirit

Spirit is what connects us to that higher power we all believe in, whether we call it God or the universe.

EXPLORING AREAS OF LIFE THROUGH NEUROLOGICAL LEVEL ALIGNMENT

In NLP we can explore an area of life and experience some new insight into it and transform our experience of it.

Exercise:

We choose an area of our life that we would like to explore and then stand somewhere with at least six feet of empty space in front of us and lay down 6 cards about 1 step apart on the floor extending out in front of us.

Each one of the cards will be spatially anchored as follows:

- Environment
- Behaviours
- Capabilities
- Values and Beliefs
- Identity
- Spirit

Each level will give you a new perspective on the area of life you have chosen to explore.

We step into the first space marked 'Environment' and we think about our environment, what we see hear and feel when we engage in that area of our lives, Who is with us and who isn't.

Then we step into the second space, marked 'Behaviour' and we think about our behaviour, thoughts and states, when we engage in that area of our life and what we say do and think, how we behave in general.

Then we step into the third space, marked 'Capabilities' and we think about our capabilities when we engage in that area of our life, our resources and skills, our knowledge, what we are capable of.

Then we step into the space marked 'Beliefs and Values' and we think about our beliefs and values and what we stand for when we engage in that area of our life, what is true to us what is important or necessary.

Then we step forward into the space marked 'Identity' and we think about our identity, who we are when we engage in that area of our life.

And finally we take a step into the space of Spirit, and we think about what connects us to the rest of the universe, what is it that we consider a higher power, what drives us and gives us purpose in life and we think about our highest intent and purpose.

Then with that sense of connectedness and purpose we turn and face back down the way we came and we bring that new perspective and all that sense of awareness and purpose back into the space of identity and we think about how that higher power and purpose, that drive determining our identity and giving us a new perspective on who we are and we notice how that ties in with the area of life we have chosen to work on.

Then we step into the space of 'beliefs and values' and we have a new perspective on whats important or necessary and we think about how that higher power and sense of purpose that drives our identity determines what we believe and value in life and we notice how that ties in with the area of life we have chosen to work on.

Then we step back into the space of capabilities and we bring to it a new perspective on the resources and skills we can make use of and we think about how our values and beliefs determine what we are capable of in some way, giving us the opportunity to prepare ourselves for life and we notice how that ties in with the area of life we have chosen to work on.

We then step back into the space of behaviour bringing with us a new perspective of what is possible, of our capabilities and new values and beliefs and we find ourselves behaving differently, thinking differently and having new states and we think about our behaviour and how we behave, what it is we think say and do driven by our sense of purpose and our beliefs and what we are capable of and we notice how that ties in with the area of life we have chosen to work on.

And finally we step back into the space of environment again with all that we have learnt about ourselves and bringing with us that new perspective of life and what we are capable of and our new behaviours and we think about our environment in a new light, we see it more clearly and we live it fully knowing that we can make changes to it driven by our sense of self and our connectedness, our new beliefs and capabilities and we notice how that ties in with the area of life we have chosen to work on.

We can take notes of what we have learned and experienced, and we may find the changes and insights continue to come for hours and sometimes days afterward.

CHANGING A PROBLEM USING NEUROLOGICAL LEVELS

We can also use Neurological Level Alignment to work on problems, changing them in a fundamental way.

Exercise:

We choose a problem we've had that we would like to change and we stand somewhere with at least six feet of empty space in front of us and we lay down 6 cards about 1 step apart on the floor extending out in front of us.

Each one of the cards will be spatially anchored as follows:

- Environment
- Behaviours
- Capabilities
- Values and Beliefs
- Identity
- Spirit

Each level will give you a new perspective on the problem you have chosen to work on.

We first take a step forward into Environment and we think of the environment where the problem occurs, we think about what we see hear and feel, who else is there, we think about what is in the foreground but also what the background holds for us and we think about what we could change that may solve the problem.

Then we take another step forward into Behaviour and we think about our behaviour, our thoughts and states and we consider what we actually do and say and think in the problem situation and we think about what we could change that may solve the problem, how a new behaviour, new thoughts and states could make a big difference.

We take another step forward into Capabilities and we think about what capabilities we have, what resources and skills we possess and what resources and skills we may not be making full use of, we think also about any resources we may not have tapped into and anything in the background that we may not have seen and we think about what we could change that may solve the problem, how new capabilities, resources and skills may make a big difference.

Then we take another step forward into Values and Beliefs and we think about what beliefs we are acting on in that situation, what we value and what is true to us about that situation, we think about what is important or necessary to us. We think about the situation we want to change and consider a change in values and beliefs, and we consider a change in what we find important or necessary and we think about what we could change that may solve the problem.

We then take another step forward into Identity and think about Who we are in this situation? What kind of person are we in this situation and maybe also who we want to be and what would we like to change about that, we consider changing who we are and we think about what we could change that may solve the problem.

Then we take another step forward, and remember that we are here for a reason and that the problem presented itself because we're meant to learn something and that we are connected to something greater than ourselves whether we believe in God, the universe and the laws of nature, consciousness, beingness, or humanity and that it is a vast source of energy so we take another step forward into that source of energy and feel connected, we feel a sense of awareness and purpose that drives us and we consider a new approach to the problem and we think about how this new energy, this new perspective can affect us through every level from identity right down to environment.

With that new sense of awareness, purpose and connectedness we turn around and take one step back into Identity and we notice how our identity transforms changing that sense of who we are.

We take another step back into Values and Beliefs and we notice how that new sense of awareness, purpose and connectedness changes our values and beliefs changing what we consider important or necessary.

We take another step backwards into Capabilities and we notice how that new sense of awareness, purpose and connectedness changes our capabilities with new resources and skills we didn't know we had.

We take another step backwards into Behaviours and we notice how that new sense of awareness, purpose and connectedness changes our behaviours our thoughts and our states making us more prepared for a positive outcome. We change what we say and do and we find ourselves behaving differently.

We take another step backwards into Environment and are aware of how our actions change the Environment around us and the situation changes and is no longer a problem and we notice how that new sense of awareness, purpose and connectedness changes our environment.

ACHIEVING OUTCOMES USING NEUROLOGICAL LEVELS

We can also use Neurological Level Alignment to help us achieve an Outcome.

Exercise:

We think of an outcome, something we would like to achieve.

We stand somewhere with at least six feet of empty space in front of us and we lay down 6 cards about 1 step apart on the floor extending out in front of us.

Each one of the cards will be spatially anchored as follows:

- Environment
- Behaviours
- Capabilities
- Values and Beliefs
- Identity
- Spirit

Each level will give you a different aspect/perspective of the outcome you have chosen to work on.

We first step into Environmental and think about the environment we are in and of all that we see hear feel and we think of all the visible resources we have at the time and what we can do with what we have at our reach, we consider both the foreground and the background and anything we haven't allowed ourself to perceive before that might contribute to achieving the outcome.

We then step into Behaviours and we think about our behaviour, our thoughts, and states while in that environment, the state we allow ourself to be in is important here and we think of the types of behaviour we will need to achieve our outcome. We think of our state, thoughts, attitude our posture, breathing and the way we speak and move and how they might contribute to achieving the outcome.

We then step into Capabilities and we think of all the resources we have, all the skills and knowledge we possess as well as all the strengths and abilities and how they might contribute to achieving the outcome..

We then step into Values and Beliefs and we think of all the values and beliefs we hold, of the limiting beliefs we might have to deal with and of all the enabling and supportive beliefs we will need to achieve our outcome. We think of what we hold true and what we stand for and how it might contribute to achieving the outcome.

We then step into Identity and we think of who we are in this environment and about who we need to become to achieve our outcome, how becoming someone that we are not might contribute to achieving the outcome.

We then step into Spirit and we think about our hightest intent, our purpose, what drives us and we think about the positive legacy our contributions will leave for mankind and posterity and with all the power and energy that drives us and connects us with the world at this level we turn around facing the opposite direction on the floor.

We then step back into identity and we think about how our highest purpose and intent will be driving and modifying who we are as a person and our connectedness with others, deeply shaping who we are in powerful ways and we think of how to more powerfully engage with the world to achieve our outcome.

Then we step back into Values and Beliefs and we think about how our values and beliefs have changed driven by the new person that we are and how this will aid in the pursuit of our outcome.

Then we step back into Capabilities and we think about all the new possibilities that have arisen from our change of identity and the change of our values and beliefs, we feel confident that with our new skills and knowledge we will be able to achieve our outcome.

Then we step back into Behaviours and we think about how our behaviour has changed. We are now in a more powerful state with powerful thoughts and enabling beliefs that will support us in achieving our outcome. Our performance serves now the pursuit of our outcome.

And Finally we step back into Environment and we think about how our environment has changed, we see it differently, and we bring to it all that we have learned all that we have gained throughout the various other levels and we take in all that is around us both in the foreground and in the background becoming more aware of our surroundings and of the many resources around us and the people around us and we notice who is there and who is no longer there.

We are now ready to achieve our outcome and we thank the power of Spirit for empowering us throughout the different levels and driving the new identity to achieve the outcome.

This is a very powerful exercises that can be used to finish off a chain of NLP interventions, because it reinforces and integrates learnings covering the gamut across all levels of experience.

SPREADING LOVE AND LIGHT TO THE WORLD

In your mind's eye imagine or represent a sphere of light of about 10cm in diameter holding itself idle right in front of you.

Hold it in your hands and bring it closer to you.

Breath Love and Energy into it and see it getting bigger and brighter 3D pulsating.

Make it bigger and bigger and bigger and bigger as you watch it get brighter and brighter and brighter.

Let it go and watch it spread and dissipate into the world around you. :D

References

George Faddoul, iNLP Practitioner Training, Quantum Change Seminars, 2007

Tim Hallbom – NLP Master Practitioner Manual, 2007

Further Reading

George Faddoul - *How To Get A Bigger Bite Out Of Life, Quantum Change Publishing, 1996*

George Faddoul - *Modern Day Alchemist, Quantum Change Publishing, 2009*

George Faddoul - *The Evolution of iNLP, Quantum Change Publishing, 2012*

George Faddoul - *101 Million Dollar Marketing Ideas, Quantum Change Publishing, 2012*

George Faddoul - *Unlocking Your Ideal Weight, Quantum Change Publishing, 2015*

Dr. Jamie Fettig - *Creaters Manual For Your Body, Quantum Change Publishing, 2004*

Steven Covey – *The Seven Habit's of Highly Effective People, Simon & Schuster, 1989*

Richard Bandler and John Grinder – *Frogs Into Princess, Real People Press, 1981*

Joseph O'Connor – *NLP Workbook, Harper Collins, 2001*

Judith DeLosier and John Grinder – *Turtles All the Way Down, Grinder & Assoc, 1995*

Judy Bartkowiak – *Secrets of the NLP Masters, 2014*

Richard Bandler and Will MacDonald, *An Insider's Guide To Sub-Modalities, Meta Publications, 1988*

William Morrow, *Technology of Achievement, 1994*

Steve and Connirae Andreas: *Heart of the Mind, Real People Press, 1987*

Connirae and Tamara Andreas: *Core Transformation, Real People Press, 1994*

Richard Bandler and John Grinder: *Structure of Magic Vol. 1, Science and Behaviour Books, 1975*

Richard Bandler and John Grinder: *Structure of Magic Vol. 2, Science and Behaviour Books, 1976*

Richard Bandler and Virginia Satir: Changing With Families, Science and Behaviour Books, 1976

Richard Bandler and Will MacDonald: An Insider's Guide to Sub-Modalities, Meta Publications, 1988

Leslie Cameron-Bandler: Solutions, Real People Press, 1985

Leslie Cameron-Bandler, D. Gordon and M. Lebeau: Emotional Hostage, Real People Press, 1986

Judith Delozier and John Grinder: Turtles all the Way Down, Meta Publications, 1987

Robert Dilts and T Epstein: Dynamic Learning, Meta Publications, 1997

Robert Dilts: Roots of NLP, Meta Publications, 1983

Robert Dilts, Richard Bandler, Judith Delozier, Leslie Cameron-Bandler and John Grinder: NLP Vol. 1, Meta Publications, 1979

Robert Dilts, Tim Hallbom, Suzi Smith: Beliefs. Pathways to Health and Well-Being, Metamorphous Press, 1990

Robert Dilts: Modelling with NLP, Meta Publications, 1999

Robert Dilts, Judith Delozier: Encyclopedia of NLP, NLP University Press, 2000

Robert Dilts: Sleight of Mouth, Meta Publications, 1999

Robert Dilts: Changing Belief systems, Meta Publications, 1990

Robert Dilts: Strategies of Genius, Meta Publications, 1995-1996

Nick LeForce: Healing the Hurts of the Heart: Breaking the Shackles of Emotional Debt, 1998

Biography

Hi, My name is Ana and I live in Sydney Australia with my little dog Happy.

I'm a new author and this is my first book.

My book is non-fiction and I write about NLP (Neurolinguistic Programming) as I truly enjoyed studying NLP and now I wish to share what I have learnt with others.

I believe that "Anything that engages people is worth doing"

The best way to describe NLP is: "NLP is the epistemology of returning to what we have lost – a state of grace." John Grinder

My Mission or Goal is Evolutionary Mindsetting

My Vision or Outcome is that of a Better World, one that improves and evolves without hostility. This is Our Greatest Legacy

Ana

Printed in the United States
By Bookmasters